Half Yard™
Bags & Purses

Half Yard™
Bags & Purses

Sew 12 beautiful bags and
12 matching purses

Debbie Shore

SEARCH PRESS

First published in 2018

Search Press Limited
Wellwood, North Farm Road,
Tunbridge Wells, Kent TN2 3DR

Reprinted 2018

Photographs by Garie Hind

ISBN: 978-1-78221-460-1

For further inspiration:
- join the Half Yard Sewing Club:
www.halfyardsewingclub.com
- visit Debbie's YouTube channel:
www.youtube.com/user/thimblelane
- visit Debbie's website:
www.debbieshoresewing.com

Suppliers
For details of suppliers, please visit the
Search Press website: www.searchpress.com

Printed in China by 1010 Printing International Ltd

Acknowledgements

Thank you, Becky Robbins, for editing
my growing library of books, for
remaining excited about the projects
and organizing my bombardments of
words and pictures when I'm on a roll!
Thanks also to Melissa Nayler, my right-
hand girl and sewing buddy, whose
honest opinion on my projects and
techniques I truly value.

Most of all thanks to you who buy my
books, give amazing feedback and
encourage me to keep writing more!

Contents

Casual Tassel Bag, page 26

Casual Tassel Purse, page 31

Working Girl Tote, page 58

Working Girl Wallet, page 64

First Class Caddy, page 68

First Class Passport Wallet, page 74

Blooming Marvellous Tote, page 104

Blooming Marvellous Purse, page 108

Twisted Threads Bag, page 112

Twisted Threads Purse, page 116

QR-CODED VIDEOS:

Introduction

Whether it's lunch with friends, a work day, dinner out or a walk in the park, there will probably be a bag of some sort over your shoulder! Make your own and you'll have the perfect bag for every occasion, large or small, plain or patterned. In this book I'll show you how to create bags for the beach, office, theatre and more, and each bag has a matching purse so that you're always coordinated! You can choose from very simple projects such as the Casual Tassel Bag and Purse (see pages 26–33), or those that require a little more sewing skill such as the First Class Caddy (see page 68–73) and the Crafty Girl's Purse (see pages 98–103). And don't worry if you're a beginner – there are plenty of pictures to show you what to do and clear, jargon-free instructions to follow.

Each bag is made with no more than half a yard of outer fabric: you'll need to add your lining, zips, fasteners and straps on top of that. To keep my fabric requirements within half a yard for each piece I haven't added too many pockets, but any bag with a lining could benefit from a 'letterbox' zip (see pages 22–23 for step-by-step instructions and a QR video link). Or you could add patch pockets to either the inside or outside of the bag if the design allows. Personalize the bags and purses as much as you like! Lengthen the handles, add appliqué and embellishments such as buttons and bows, and experiment with fabrics. Just make sure you use a ¼in (5mm) seam allowance unless otherwise stated.

I've added QR-coded videos to this book to help you with some of the sewing techniques. To view the videos, you'll need a smartphone and a barcode application (the majority of these are free). Once you've installed it, use the phone's camera to scan the barcode, which will automatically load the video...

Debbie

10 tips for the complete beginner

1 Start with a relatively simple project such as the Cocktail Hour Purse (see pages 90–93). As your skills grow, you'll feel confident to tackle more advanced bags.

2 Make up your bag or purse in an inexpensive fabric first; that way, if things go wrong, you're not wasting anything but time!

3 Measure twice, cut once: stitches can be unpicked but if you don't cut the right size there's little you can do.

4 Reverse a couple of stitches at the start and end of your sewing line. Some machines have a 'fix' stitch that puts three or four tiny stitches close together. This will stop the stitches coming undone.

5 Cut your fabric pieces on the grain – this means that the weave of the fabric sits vertically and horizontally; if you cut at an angle (on the bias) your fabric could twist.

6 To help keep your sewn lines straight and your seams even, place a strip of masking tape over the bed of your sewing machine as a guide for your fabric; an elastic band around the free arm works well too. Measure from the needle ¼in (5mm) to the right and place your tape at this point.

7 Top-stitching can be a bit daunting – if you're not very confident, sew slowly and use a thread that matches your fabric so that it doesn't stand out too much.

8 Pin at right angles to the edge of your fabric. You'll find the layers don't slip and, although you should be taking out your pins as you sew, if the needle accidentally hits a pin there is less chance of either breaking.

9 Change your sewing-machine needle regularly – it's recommended you put a new needle in after every eight hours of sewing – as you'll notice a difference to the stitches and even the sound of your machine! It's always good form when you change the needle to take off the needle plate and clear out any lint (take a look at your manufacturer's instructions).

10 Relax – sewing is fun! Don't worry if things go a bit wrong, simply put your work down and come back to it the next day – it won't seem half as bad as you thought!

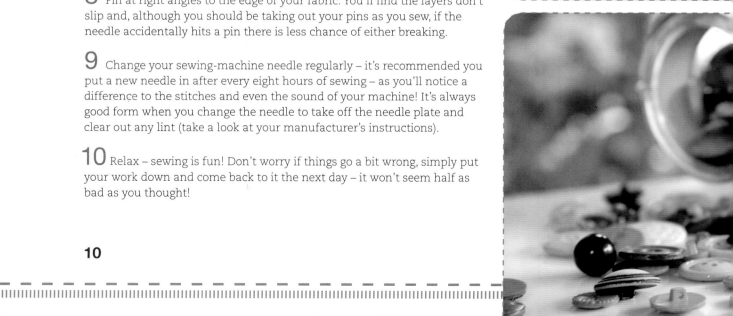

Sewing kit

FABRIC

The fabric you use for your bag is entirely your choice, but here are a few things you might want to consider before you commit to buying. A finer fabric such as quilting or craft cotton will benefit from stabilizer or interfacing on the wrong side to add extra firmness. A home-décor fabric will be heavier and may not need interfacing, but feel the drape of the fabric when you buy – a floppy fabric will create a floppy bag! Use a woven interfacing on the back of knitted fabrics like jersey, to stop the stretch.

THREADS

Always use a superior-quality thread. They are usually more expensive but are worth the investment as they are generally stronger, too. As your bag will be taking weight it's important that the seams don't give way. If you pull the thread and it snaps easily in your fingers, chances are it will snap easily in your seams.

HABERDASHERY

Buttons, ribbons, lace, buckles and zips are fun and practical notions to embellish your bags and purses, and can help to give them a shop-bought look. Many fabric ranges include bindings and ribbons to provide a perfect colour match. A cleverly placed button can easily disguise a wobbly stitch!

HARDWARE

Metalwork gives a bag a professional, shop-bought look, and there are many fastenings, rings, clasps and chains available to choose from. There are rectangular, swivel and D-rings for attaching straps, and sliders to make them adjustable. There are locks and magnetic clasps to fasten your bags and feet to protect the bases. All of them are used in this book and feel free to add more if you wish!

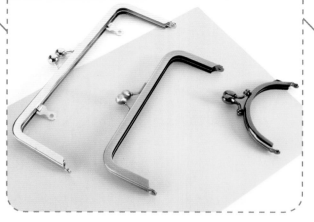

FRAMES

You can choose from a wide variety of shapes and sizes of frames to create your own unique purse. Sew-in frames (shown right) have holes around the frame to stitch through, so use strong thread to help stop breakage. Glue-in frames (above) need a strong wet glue to secure the top of the purse into the frame – glue one side at a time, leaving the first side to dry before moving on to the second.

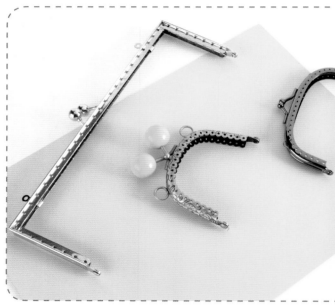

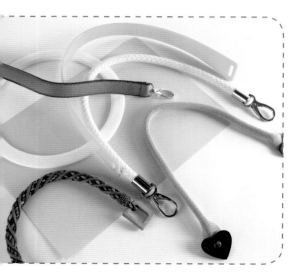

HANDLES

I made my own straps and handles for the Ladies' Day Bag (page 78) and for the Working Girl Tote (page 58), but you may find it easier to buy handles instead. Some clip on, so you'll need a ring to attach them, some are sewn on and for some you'll need to make a fabric loop. Have fun experimenting!

WEBBING

This is probably the easiest possible way to make a strap, and here's a tip: to stop the ends from fraying, carefully hold the end of the webbing over the flame of a candle to singe it; alternatively, sew across the end with a zigzag stitch. I used webbing for the First Class Caddy on page 68.

BAG BASE

This is a sturdy plastic strip that will sit between the outer and lining base pieces of your bag to provide a firmer shape. The mesh is useful if you're adding feet – it's easy to push the feet through and it helps to secure the base in place.

SCISSORS

For cutting fabric you'll need dressmaking shears: I use 10in (25.5cm) shears with angled handles, which help to keep the fabric flat as you're cutting it. Pinking shears are useful for snipping into seam allowances, a small pair of scissors is useful for snipping threads, and you'll also want a pair of paper scissors for cutting out patterns.

MARKING PENS

You can choose from heat-, water- or air-erasable pens, but be careful not to iron over water- or air-erasable types as the ink will set and become permanent. I prefer heat-erasable; always test on a patch of scrap fabric first as the ink can fade the print on some fabrics.

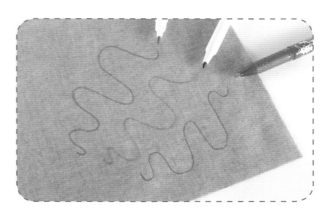

SEWING MACHINE

You don't need a fancy machine for the projects in this book, as only straight, zigzag and over-edge stitches are used. If you're buying for the first time you'll find a computerized machine easy to use, and some have a speed control and start/stop button so a foot pedal isn't required to sew. Look for a machine with a needle up/down facility, and a needle threader, and go for a named brand – it's important to have support and a guarantee in case anything goes wrong.

PINS AND FABRIC CLIPS

I prefer flower- or glass-head pins, as I can see them both in the fabric and on the floor when I drop them! Fabric clips are a great alternative for thicker fabrics that can't be pinned.

IRON

Although I mostly use a steam iron for pressing my projects I find a little travel iron so useful for quick pressing next to my sewing machine or for making bias binding.

BIAS BINDING TOOL

Available in different sizes, you feed your fabric through this tool to create folded binding. This is the easiest way to make your own bias binding (see page 18). I use the 1in (2.5cm) tool most frequently.

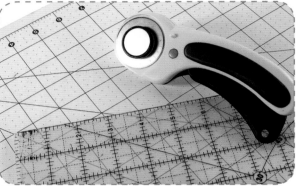

ROTARY CUTTER, RULER AND MAT

These tools are essential for cutting straight lines, particularly through layers of fabrics. Choose a 45mm rotary cutter, a 6 x 24in (15.25 x 61cm) ruler and a mat as large as you have room for. Some mats are double-sided, with both metric and imperial markings, and you'll find 60- and 45-degree lines useful.

HOLE PUNCH

Invest in a punch with several sized holes, as this simple tool gives you accurate holes for threading or attaching snaps. You'll find an awl (or poking tool) useful to poke out the inside of the holes.

EYELETS AND PUNCH

Available in many sizes and colours, eyelets can be used decoratively, for clipping on handles (see the Cocktail Hour Bag on pages 86–89) or threading cord (see the All Decked Out Bag on pages 34–37). Follow the manufacturer's instructions – you may need a small hammer to punch out the holes.

ADHESIVES

Buy a repositionable spray adhesive to secure appliqué pieces or to bond wadding/batting to your fabric. A strong wet fabric glue is important for gluing in purse frames (see the Ladies' Day Purse on page 83) and felt (see the Girl About Town Bag on page 40). A dot of glue behind a button can help keep it secured.

TAILOR'S HAM/SEAM ROLL

Use this for pressing, when pressing flat isn't an option! Push the ham into bag bases to iron them while keeping the bag's shape.

Before you start

Machine stitches

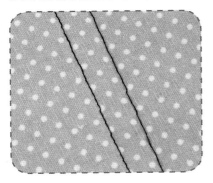

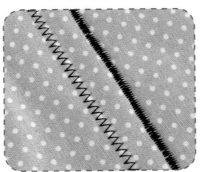

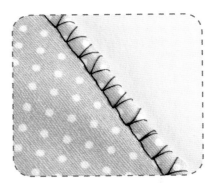

STRAIGHT STITCH

This is the most-used stitch on any project. Lengthen the thread to create a tacking/basting stitch and, if you loosen the tension, it's easy to pull the bottom thread to gather your fabric.

ZIGZAG STITCH

A decorative stitch that can be used to join two pieces of fabric together to create a flat seam, this stitch can also be useful to help stop the raw edges of your fabric from fraying. Shorten the length of the stitch to make a satin stitch – perfect for edging appliqué shapes.

OVER-EDGE STITCH

This is designed to take the thread slightly over the raw edge of your fabric to stop it from fraying (it is similar to an overlock stitch, which is produced by an overlocker/serger). Use this on items that may wear or need to be laundered; if you sell your items this will give them a professional finish.

Hand stitches

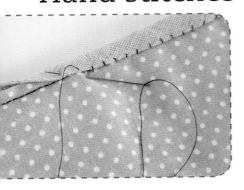

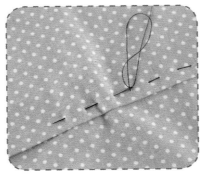

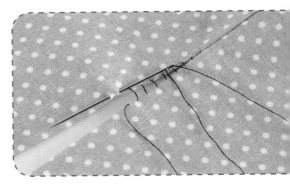

SLIP STITCH

I use this to finish off bias binding (see page 18). Keep the stitch to a short length and try to catch just a couple of strands of the fold of the bias binding to keep the stitch as invisible as possible.

RUNNING STITCH

Use this in the same way as a machine straight stitch (if tiny, the stitches can be just as strong). It can be used as a tacking/basting stitch, and the stitches can be pulled to gather the fabric.

LADDER STITCH

The perfect stitch for closing turning gaps or making repairs in seams: take the needle from one side of the opening to the opposite side, then gently pull to close the gap. Small stitches are the least visible.

Cutting into curves

For curves that are to be turned, make little V-shaped cuts into the fabric up to the seam – this will stop the fabric from puckering when turned. You could also use pinking shears for the same effect.

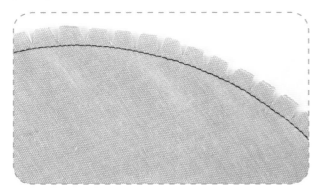

Cutting corners

This helps to keep the corners square when turned the right way out. Cut away the corner, keeping as close to the stitches as you can without snipping them.

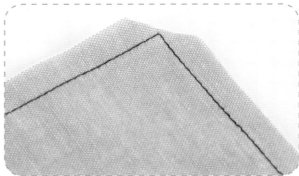

Piping

A strip of piping around a bag or across a pocket gives a professional finishing touch to your work, and is simple to make for yourself. Cord comes in many different sizes: I'd use a fine cord on pockets, and up to ¼in (5mm) cord for bag seams.

1 Cut your fabric into strips, wide enough to wrap around the cord and go under the sewing-machine needle. If you're taking the piping around a curve, then cut the fabric strips on the bias. Pin the raw edges together, sandwiching the cord in the centre.

2 Using the zipper foot on your machine, sew alongside the cord, making sure the raw edges are together. Take out the pins as you sew.

3 To apply to your fabric, sandwich the piping between the two pieces of fabric, right sides and raw edges together, then sew with your zipper foot (piping feet are available for some sewing machines).

VIDEO
Piping

Fabric straps

There are just two types of fabric straps for you to make in this book, open-ended and closed-ended. The open-ended straps are sewn into the top seams of your bag, the closed-ended straps are sewn to the front of your bag. Add interfacing or fusible fleece to the wrong side of your fabric strips if you need a stiffer handle, or a blast of spray starch can give a crisp finish to your straps. You can make the straps shorter if needed just by cutting off some of the length, or extend them.

OPEN-ENDED STRAP

1 Cut out your fabric. Fold in half lengthways and press.

2 Fold the two long sides to the centre and press.

3 Fold in half again and press.

4 Top-stitch along both long sides.

CLOSED-ENDED STRAP

Start by following steps 1–3 as above.

4 Fold the long sides of the strap together so that the raw edges are on the outside. Sew across the bottom.

5 Turn right side out and then top-stitch neatly all around the edge.

Bias binding

I use quite a lot of bias binding in my projects as it's a simple way to finish off raw edges and gives a professional finish to your work. Although it can be bought in many colours and sizes, I like to make my own. It's not only cost-effective, but it also means I can coordinate it with my fabrics. Bias tape is so called as it's a strip of fabric cut at a 45-degree angle (on the bias). This allows a little 'give' so the fabric stretches around curves without puckering.

VIDEO

Cutting and folding bias binding

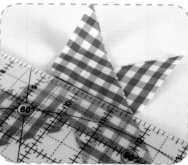

1 Lay your fabric squarely on the cutting mat and, using the 45-degree mark, place the ruler along the straight edge of the fabric. And cut! Turn your fabric over, and use the straight side of the ruler to measure the width you need. For a ½in (1cm) finished width of tape you'll need to cut 2in (5cm) wide strips of fabric. As you're cutting the strips your cut line will become longer, so fold the fabric in half, matching up the diagonal edges, and cut through two, three or four layers at a time.

2 To join the strips together, lay two pieces right sides together, overlapping at right angles. Draw a diagonal line from one corner to the other, as in the photograph. Pin, then sew along this line. Trim the seam allowance back to around ⅛in (2mm) and press the seam open.

3 Bias binding is made by folding both of the long edges of the tape into the centre and pressing. The easiest way to do this is to use a small bias tape maker, through which you thread the tape. It folds the strip in two and you press with your iron while pulling the fabric through. If you don't have a tape maker, carefully fold both long edges to the centre of the fabric strips and press. Be careful not to get your fingers too close to the iron!

4 To apply the binding, firstly open up the crease lines and, right sides together, pin across the raw edge of your work. Sew with your machine along the upper crease mark.

5 Fold the tape over the raw edge, and use slip stitch to sew by hand.

Tip

If you're applying the bias tape continuously, start by folding over the end of the tape, then pin and machine sew as in step 4. When you get back to the start, overlap the end of the tape by about 5mm (¼in). Fold over and stitch as in step 5, or instead of slip stitching by hand you could machine top-stitch.

Creating mitred corners

1 Sew along the upper crease line but stop ¼in (5mm) from the end of your work and reverse a couple of stitches.

2 Pinch the corner of the tape, matching up the raw edge with the second side of fabric.

3 Start sewing at the edge of the fabric, again along the crease line.

4 Fold the tape over and you'll see a neat fold in the corner.

5 When you've finished sewing the bias tape to the front, pin the corner, then hand sew on the back.

Fitting a magnetic clasp

These simple clasps don't usually come with instructions, so here's how to fit them. I'd recommend placing a scrap of fabric behind the clasp, on the wrong side of your fabric, to stabilize the fabric and help to stop the clasp pulling. If you're fitting to a bag with a flap, the thinner side of the clasp will go on the flap and the thicker section on the bag.

1 Mark the position of the clasp with an erasable ink pen – take the clasp backing plate and draw through the two long holes.

2 Use your quick-unpick or a small pair of sharp scissors to make a small incision at each line. It's better to make the cuts too small, as they can easily be made bigger – if you cut them too big you may ruin your project.

3 Push the clasp prongs through the holes, through a scrap of fabric and through the backing plate. Open out the prongs on the back of the fabric. It doesn't really matter whether you open them outwards or close them inwards – personally I find them easier to open outwards.

4 Repeat for the other half of the clasp.

Adding a twist fastening

A twist fastening looks professional and stylish, but most importantly adds an extra level of security to your bag. I used it on my Cocktail Hour Bag (see pages 86–89). If you are using this in another design, check how wide the side pieces will be to ensure you position the flap correctly.

1 On the back of the flap, measure up from the centre bottom of the lining as per your instructions (here, 2in/5cm) and mark: place the 'hole' side of the twist lock over the top, and draw around the inside. Also mark where the screws will go.

2 Carefully cut around this shape, and into the markings where the screws will go. You'll have to trim a tiny amount away, but this needs to be a snug fit around the clasp with no gaps, so take your time and only snip away a little at a time.

3 Push the top piece of the lock through from the front side. When you're happy with the fit, drizzle a tiny amount of fabric glue around the hole to secure it.

4 Pop the second, rear part of the lock over the top and screw in the screws to secure it.

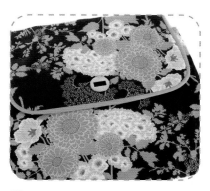

5 Place the flap centrally over the front side of the bag, with the top of the flap overhanging the top of the bag by 2in (5cm) – this amount may vary from project to project, depending on how deep your bag will be. Mark through the hole for the position of the lock.

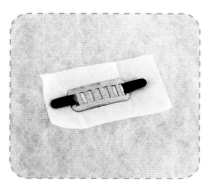

6 Pop a piece of interfacing over the back of the front panel of the bag, then make two small incisions for the 'legs' of the lock to go through. Push the legs through all layers from the right side, slip on the backing plate and open out the legs to secure.

Adding pockets

Most of the bags in this book would benefit from an inside pocket or two, either a patch pocket with an open top to help organize the contents of your bag (see below), or fitted into the lining and closed with a zip to make it secure (see pages 22–23).

PATCH POCKETS

Adding a patch pocket to either the inside or outside of your bag is quick and simple. You can make a patch pocket any size you like – long and thin or wide and square – and it can be divided into sections to hold anything from phones to pens. Adding a strip of bias binding across the top creates a decorative trim, and you could fasten the top edge with a button or magnetic clasp if you wish.

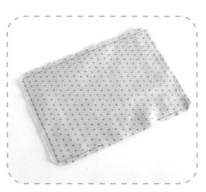

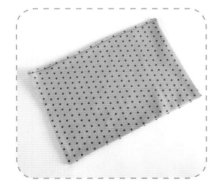

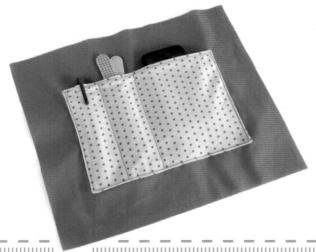

1 Cut two pieces of fabric measuring ½in (1cm) larger than the finished size you require.

2 Sew right sides together all the way round, leaving a turning gap in the bottom. The size of the gap depends on how small your pocket is, but should ideally be about 3in (7.5cm) in length. Snip off the corners of the pocket – this will reduce bulk when turned through and make the corners sharper.

3 Turn right side out and press. Top-stitch across the top edge of the pocket.

4 Pin in place to either the lining or outer bag fabric, then sew around the bottom and sides. As you sew across the bottom, the turning gap will close. To reinforce the seam, either backstitch a couple of stitches at the start and end of your sewing, or sew a small triangle shape each side at the top of the pocket.

5 Decide if you need to divide the pocket. If so, measure and mark the dividing lines and sew, remembering to backstitch at each end.

LETTERBOX ZIPPED POCKETS

The letterbox zipped pocket is fitted into the lining before the bag is constructed and can be made any size you like, within the size of the lining. I prefer to use nylon zips, as they can be cut to size. Note that some bags, such as the Twisted Threads Bag (see pages 112–115) aren't suitable for this type of pocket, as the lining is gathered.

VIDEO
Making a letterbox zip

1 Cut two pieces of fabric to the size of the pocket you need. This should be shorter than your bag lining fabric, and can either be the same width, so that the pocket is sewn into the side seam, or narrower than the bag. Choose a zip that is a couple of inches longer than the pocket opening – it will sit flatter when the ends with the metal stoppers are cut off. I like to use continuous zipping, as I can cut it to any length I like.

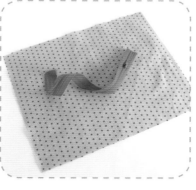
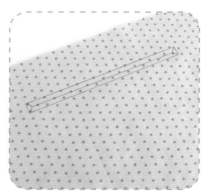

2 Draw a rectangle onto the wrong side of a pocket lining piece, in the position you'd like the zip, measuring ½in (1cm) wide, and the length of the zip opening. Draw another line straight through the centre of the box, with a 'Y' shape at each end going into the corners of the rectangle.

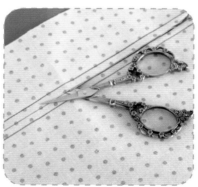

3 Pin the pocket lining right sides together to your bag lining fabric. With a small stitch on your machine, carefully sew around the zip box. Take a small sharp pair of scissors and cut along the centre line, then into the 'Y' shapes, up to, but not through the stitches.

4 Push the lining through the hole (this is why it's known as a 'letterbox' zip!) and press.

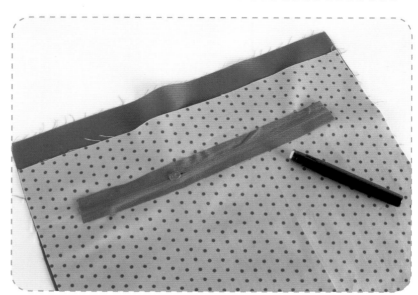

5 Place the zip behind the hole. Either tack/baste or use a temporary glue stick to hold the zip in place, then sew around the zip on your machine, moving the zip slider out of the way as you get to it, to keep your lines straight.

6 Pin the two pocket pieces right sides together, keeping the bag lining (here, the red fabric) out of the way. Sew across the top and bottom edges of the pocket lining fabric only.

7 If your pocket is going to fit into the side seams of the bag, you only need to sew across the top and bottom of the pocket. Tack/baste the pocket to the sides of the lining, or sew with a narrow seam allowance. Remove the pins.

8 If your pocket is narrower than the width of the lining, sew the sides of the two pocket lining pieces as well, again avoiding the red bag lining fabric.

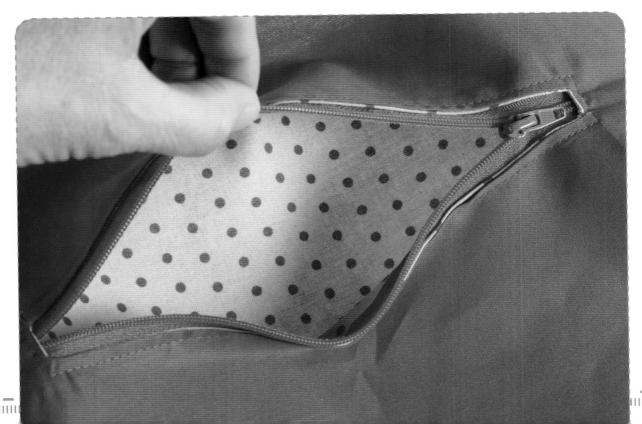

The Projects

Casual Tassel Bag

The unusual fastening on this bag makes it both unique and fun! Don't choose a fabric that is too heavy, as this bag is supposed to be soft and slouchy – my faux suede is a brushed polyester.

1 Sew the dark faux suede pocket piece right sides together with the pocket lining across the top. Fold wrong sides together. As the lining is slightly bigger it will create a border across the top of the pocket. Press then top-stitch either side of the seam.

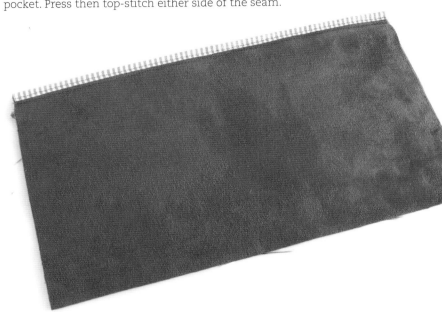

2 Add two eyelets to the pocket piece, following the manufacturer's instructions, 7½in (19cm) from the left side, 2½in (6.5cm) down from the top. Fuse or adhere the interfacing pieces to the wrong sides of the light faux suede pieces. Place the pocket over the bottom of one of these pieces, as shown below.

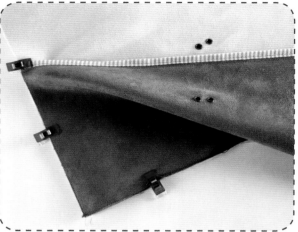

3 Clip the two sections together then mark the position of the eyelets on the light faux suede by putting the erasable ink pen through the pocket eyelets. Apply two more eyelets to these new marks.

4 Thread the 14in (35.5cm) leather cord through the eyelets, from back to front, and loosely tie.

5 Take twelve 8in (20.5cm) cut cord pieces and tie one end of the 14in (35.5cm) cord around the centre.

6 Fold the twelve cord lengths in half, then take one more length and wrap around the top of the tassel. Push the end of the cord inside the tassel and secure with a spot of wet glue. Repeat at the other end of the long cord, with another twelve short pieces.

7 Make up one more tassel using another twelve 8in (20.5cm) pieces, securing with a 7in (18cm) length of cord to tie to the side of the bag later.

8 Pop the tassels inside the pocket to keep them out of the way when sewing the rest of the bag together. To make the D-ring tabs, take the strip of fabric and fold in half lengthways, right sides together. Sew along the long open edge to make a tube. Turn right side out and press with the seam in the centre. Top-stitch along each long edge. Cut into three equal pieces.

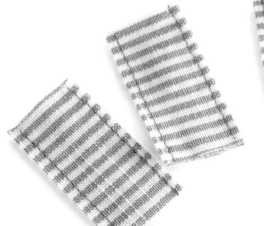

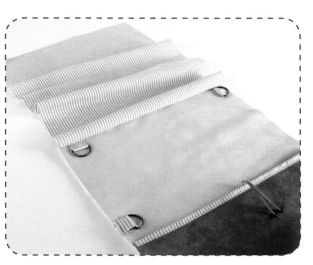

9 Thread each tab through a D-ring. Tack/baste one tab to the top right-hand side of the front of the bag, ½in (1cm) down from the top. Tack/baste a second tab to the left-hand side of the bag, 7in (17.75cm) down from the top. The third tab goes on the left-hand side of the top edge of the bag front, ½in (1cm) in from the left-hand side. All tabs should be facing inwards.

10 Sew the top of the lining pieces to the top of the bag pieces. Take care to avoid the D-rings as you sew – we don't want any broken needles!

11 Sew the two sections right sides together, lining to lining and outer to outer, leaving a turning gap of about 5in (13cm) in the bottom of the lining. Snip across the corners, turn right side out and sew the opening closed.

12 Push the lining inside the bag and press; test a scrap of faux leather first to make sure the iron won't damage it. Top-stitch around the top of the bag.

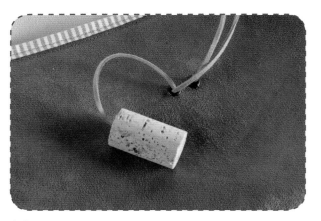
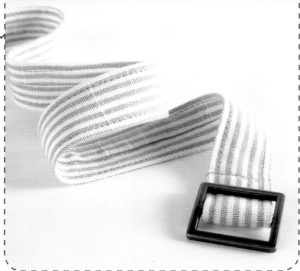

13 Make a hole in the end of the cork with an awl, pop a dot of wet glue inside and push the end of the remaining 7in (18cm) length of cord into the hole. When the glue has dried, thread the other end through one of the eyelets and knot inside the pocket.

14 To make the strap, fold the long strip of fabric in half lengthways, right sides together, and sew the open side, leaving a turning gap in the centre of about 4in (10cm). Roll the fabric so that the seam is in the centre and sew across each end. Snip off the corners, turn right side out and press. Sew the opening closed by hand then top-stitch both long edges. Thread one end over the bar in the centre of the slider and sew the end in place to secure.

15 Take the strap through the D-ring on the right of the bag, back through the slider then over to the D-ring on the bottom left of the bag. Fold over the end and sew.

16 Loop the tassel cords through the remaining D-ring and thread the cork through the loop to secure.

Tip
Instead of using a cork to fasten the bag, an old key or a wooden toggle would work just as well!

Casual Tassel Purse

Add a touch of hippy-chic style to your handbag collection with this fun, fold-over purse! Large enough to hold your phone or make-up, it could also double up as a cute evening clutch bag.

Finished size

7 x 5in (18 x 12.75cm)

What you need

16 x 9in (41 x 23cm) faux suede
16 x 11½in (41 x 29cm) lining fabric
16 x 9in (41 x 23cm) fusible interfacing
212in (544cm) leather cord
One button

Cut

Two pieces of faux suede measuring
8 x 9in (20.5 x 23cm)

Two pieces of lining measuring
8 x 9½in (20.5 x 24cm)

Two pieces of interfacing measuring
8 x 9in (20.5 x 23cm)

One piece of lining measuring
8 x 2in (20.5 x 5cm) for the strap

One length of cord measuring 30in (76cm) and
twenty-six lengths measuring 7in (18cm)

1 Fuse the interfacing to the wrong sides of the faux suede pieces. Make up the strap by folding the long edges of fabric to the centre then folding in half again. Press, then top-stitch along each side. Tack/baste each end of the strap to the sides of the front of the purse, about 5in (13cm) up from the bottom.

2 Sew the top of one lining piece right sides together to the top of the front piece. Fold the 30in (76cm) length of cord in half and tack/baste to the centre top of the back of the purse, facing inwards. Sew the top of the lining right sides together to the top.

3 Measure 1in (2.5cm) up from the bottom edge and 3in (7.5cm) in from the left-hand side of the front of the purse, and sew the button on here. Before knotting, wind your thread underneath the button a few times to form a shank.

4 Keeping the cord away from your stitch lines, sew the two panels right sides together around all four edges, making sure the seams match up. Leave a turning gap in the bottom of the lining of about 3in (7.5cm). Turn right side out and press; test your iron on a scrap of faux suede first, as you may need to use a pressing cloth. Sew the turning gap closed.

5 Push the lining inside the purse; you'll find that as the lining is slightly longer than the outer fabric it will form a border around the top. Top-stitch around this border. Make up two tassels (see steps 5–6 on page 28) and attach to the ends of the cord.

6 Slide the top of the purse under the strap, wrap the ties around the purse and wrap around the button to fasten.

Tip
You could make the strap 10in (25.5cm) long, fold in half and attach to one side, instead of across the purse, to make a wristlet.

All Decked Out Bag

Get set for summer with this nautical beach bag, in crisp white and blues with a rope handle. I can almost hear the waves crashing and smell the salty air!

Finished size

12 x 14 x 4in (30.5 x 35.5 x 10cm)

What you need

32 x 9in (81 x 23cm) striped fabric

32 x 9in (81 x 23cm) plain fabric

32 x 17½in (81 x 45cm) lining fabric (I've used the same plain outer fabric)

32 x 17½in (81 x 45cm) fusible fleece

2yd (2m) of ½in (1cm) wide cord

Eight ½in (1cm) eyelets

Embroidery thread

Sticky tape

Cut

Two pieces of striped fabric measuring
16 x 9in (40.5 x 23cm)

Two pieces of plain fabric measuring
16 x 9in (40.5 x 23cm)

Two pieces of fusible fleece measuring
16 x 17½in (40.5 x 45cm)

Two pieces of lining measuring
16 x 17½in (40.5 x 45cm)

1 Sew one plain outer fabric piece to the top of each striped piece. Press the seams open, fuse the fleece to the wrong sides, then top-stitch along either side of each seam.

2 Cut a 2in (5cm) square from each bottom corner of the outer and lining pieces.

3 Sew the outer pieces right sides together, leaving the top and the cut-out corners unsewn. Pull the corners open so that the side seams meet the base seam, and sew straight across to make the base square. Turn right side out.

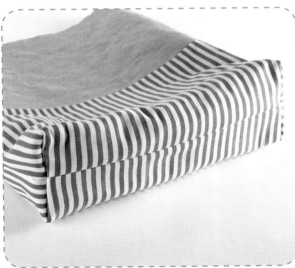

4 Repeat to sew up and box the bottom corners of the lining pieces, but this time leave a turning gap of about 5in (13cm) in the bottom seam.

5 Drop the outer bag inside the lining, right sides together. Sew around the top. Turn right side out then sew the turning gap closed.

6 Push the lining inside the bag and top-stitch around the top; lengthen your stitch length slightly. Measure and mark 1¼in (3cm) down from the top, then 1¼in (3cm) and 3½in (9cm) from each side seam. Apply an eyelet to each mark. Repeat on the other side of the bag.

7 Cut two 1yd (1m) lengths of cord. Wrap a little tape around the end of each piece to stop fraying. Thread the cord through the eyelets on each side of the bag, as in the picture below. Remove the tape.

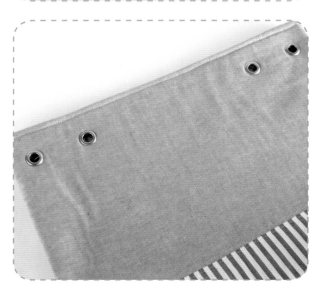

8 Wrap a length of embroidery thread around each pair of cord ends, 2in (5cm) from the end. Fray the ends. Pull the middle of the cords to form handles, then knot each side, about 6in (15cm) from the ends.

9 To make a drawstring bag, knot one side then pull the opposite side to gather the top of the bag.

Tip
Use laminated fabric for the lining if you'll be carrying damp towels.

All Decked Out Purse

This is a handy little pouch for storing anything from your sunglasses to change for ice creams! This an easy bag to resize; you'll find it useful for gifts, bottles, shoes and jewellery, or add a weight and fill with toy filler to create a stylish door stop!

Finished size

5 x 8 x 2in (12.75 x 20.5 x 5cm)

What you need

24 x 9½in (61 x 24.5cm) plain fabric
18 x 9in (46 x 23cm) striped fabric
16 x 9½in (41 x 24cm) fusible fleece
40in (102cm) of ¼in (5mm) wide cord
Large safety pin

Cut

Two pieces of plain fabric measuring
8 x 3½in (20.5 x 9cm)

Two pieces of striped fabric measuring
8 x 6½in (20.5 x 16.5cm)

Two pieces of fusible fleece measuring
8 x 9½in (20.5 x 24.5cm)

Two pieces of plain fabric for the lining
measuring 8 x 9½in (20.5 x 24.5cm)

Two pieces of striped fabric measuring
8½ x 2½in (21.5 x 6.5cm) for the
drawstring channel

Two pieces of cord each measuring
20in (51cm)

1 Sew a plain fabric piece to the top of each striped bag piece, right sides together. Press the seam open then fuse fleece to the wrong sides. Top-stitch either side of the seam.

2 Cut a 1in (2.5cm) square from the bottom corner of each outer and lining piece.

3 Take the drawstring channel pieces, fold the short ends inwards by ¼in (5mm) twice and sew. Fold in half lengthways and press.

4 Centre a channel piece raw edges and right sides together with the top of each outer bag piece and sew in place – there should be ¼in (5mm) seam allowance either side. Sew the top of the lining pieces over the top, so that the channels are trapped in between the two pieces.

5 Open out and place the two sections right sides together; pin. Sew all the way around apart from the cut-out corners, and leave a turning gap of about 3in (7.5cm) in the bottom of the lining. Match up the seams as you sew, and tuck the ends of the channel sections out of the way so you don't sew over them. Pull open the cut-out corners so that the side seams meet the base seams, and sew straight across to make the bases of both the outer and lining square. Turn right side out.

6 Sew across the opening then push the lining inside the bag and press. Top-stitch around the top of the bag.

7 Attach the end of one piece of cord to the safety pin – you may find it easiest to wrap a piece of sticky tape around the end to stop fraying. Thread from left to right through the front channel, then back from right to left through the back channel, then remove the pin and knot the ends. Repeat with the second piece of cord in the opposite direction.

Girl About Town Bag

This striking felt bag makes a contemporary accessory for the girl about town! Make sure you use a heavy-duty felt to make the bag sturdy. The whole bag is hand sewn, and punching the stitch holes makes it a very easy bag to sew!

Finished size

12 x 11 x 5in (30.5 x 28 x 12.75cm), not including handle

What you need

18 x 31in (45.75 x 79cm) of ¼in (5mm) thick grey felt

12 x 8in (30.5 x 20.5cm) of ¼in (5mm) thick yellow felt

Orange and black jewellery twine (or fine leather cord)

Large-eyed needle

Leather hole puncher and awl

Strong wet fabric glue

Magnetic clasp

Two buttons

One buckle

Fabric clips

8in (20.5cm) circle template

Chalk pencil and ruler

Tip

Felt makes a lovely backdrop for embroidery stitches, so why not hand sew a few flowers to the front of the bag?

1 Cut two pieces of grey felt measuring 12 x 10in (30.5 x 25.5cm) for the front and back panels. Take a diagonal line from each top corner to 2in (5cm) from the bottom corners and trim.

2 Cut two pieces of grey felt measuring 5 x 10in (12.75 x 25.5cm), take a diagonal line from each top corner to 1in (2.5cm) from each bottom corner and trim as before. These are the end panels.

3 Cut a piece of grey felt measuring 3 x 8in (7.5 x 20.5cm) for the base, and two pieces of grey felt measuring 7½ x 4½in (19 x 11.5cm) for the inside pockets. Draw a chalk line ¼in (5mm) from the bottom and side edges of the pocket pieces, then punch ⅛in (2.5mm) holes around these edges, ¼in (5mm) apart. Your awl will come in handy here to poke out the punched felt. Backstitch twine through the holes, starting and stopping in the centre to disguise the ends of the twine. Apply strong fabric glue to the bottom and side edges, and secure to the side felt panels, centrally, 2in (5cm) from the top.

4 Drizzle a line of glue along both side edges of one panel, place the ends of the bag on top and leave to dry – use fabric clips to hold the pieces together. I find it easier to glue the sides together before punching the holes, and it also makes the seam stronger.

5 When the glue is dry, punch ⅛in (2.5mm) holes along the side edges, ¼in (5mm) apart. Thread orange twine over the edge of the seams, then over-edge stitch twine through the holes. When you have finished, push the ends of the twine into the seams and add a spot of glue to stop them unravelling.

6 Repeat steps 4 and 5 with the opposite side of the bag, to create a glued and stitched 'tube' of fabric.

7 Glue then sew the base in the same way (refer to step 10 for a visual).

8 Take the yellow felt and, using your 8in (20.5cm) circle template, curve each short side. Using the same size and spacing as before, punch holes all around the edge. Thread twine through the holes, starting and stopping in the centre of one curved end. To make sure both ends of the twine sit on the wrong side of the flap, punch an even number of holes.

9 Cut a strip of grey felt measuring ¾ x 12¼in (2 x 31cm) – the width of the strip depends on the size of the holes in your buckle. Using the same size and spacing as before, punch holes straight down the centre, then thread with orange twine. Add the buckle 3in (7.5cm) from one end.

10 Measure and mark 1in (2.5cm) in from the centre of the curved end without the knotted thread, then attach the thin half of the magnetic clasp to the wrong side. Glue the strip over the centre of the yellow flap, covering the back of the magnetic clasp. Trim the strip if necessary. Apply glue to the back of the yellow flap – the opposite end to the clasp – up to 4in (10cm) from the curved edge. Position this over the back of the bag, centrally, 5in (13cm) from the top of the bag. As the flap isn't weight-bearing, glue is sufficient to attach it.

11 Fold the flap over the bag, mark the position of the magnetic clasp, then apply the second half – the back of the clasp should sit behind an inside pocket.

12 Cut a length of grey felt for the handle measuring 1½ x 20in (4 x 51cm). Glue to each side of the bag, 1½in (4cm) from the top, then sew a button to either side, sewing straight through both layers of felt. You could miss off the buttons and sew a large cross stitch instead. The ¼in (5mm) felt is very sturdy, but if you're concerned you could use webbing instead.

Girl About Town Purse

This simple hand-sewn felt purse could equally double as a stylish evening clutch – the bold blocks of colour create quite a 1960s feel.

Finished size

10 x 5½in (25.5 x 14cm)

What you need

10 x 11in (25.5 x 28cm) ¼in (5mm) thick grey felt

9½ x 8in (24 x 20.5cm) ¼in (5mm) thick yellow felt

Black and orange jewellery twine (or fine leather cord)

Large-eyed needle

14in (35.5cm) nylon zip

9in (23cm) circle template

Leather hole puncher and awl

Strong wet fabric glue

Magnetic clasp

Button

Fabric clips

Chalk pencil and ruler

1 Cut a 10in (25.5cm) square of grey felt. Draw a chalk line ¼in (5mm) from the top and bottom edges and punch ⅛in (2.5mm) holes along the lines, ¼in (5mm) apart. Place one half of the zip centrally under the holes and hand sew in place with orange jewellery twine. Hide the ends of the cord under the zip and secure with a spot of strong wet glue.

2 Sew the second half of the zip to the opposite side of the felt in the same way. Cut four pieces of grey felt measuring 1 x 1½in (2.5 x 4cm). Glue in pairs over each end of the zip, sandwiching the zip in the centre. Hold in place with fabric clips until dry, then punch holes ¼in (5mm) apart around the edge as before, and sew with jewellery twine. Tuck the ends inside the felt and glue.

3 Drizzle a line of glue along the inside of the sides of the purse and clip until dry. Chalk a line along each side, ¼in (5mm) from the edge, and punch ¹/₈in (2.5mm) holes ¼in (5mm) apart. Over-edge stitch in orange twine, keeping the ends of the twine inside the purse and, again, secure them with a dot of wet glue.

4 To make the flap, cut an arc from one short side of the yellow felt using your circle template. Using the same size and spacing as before, punch holes all around the edge, and make a running stitch with black twine. To make both ends of the twine sit under the flap, punch an even number of holes. Measure and mark 1in (2.5cm) in from the centre of the curved end and apply the slim part of the magnetic clasp, with the prongs on the upper side of the felt (see page 19).

5 Glue or sew the button over the prongs of the clasp.

6 Glue the flap to the back of the purse, centrally, 3in (7.5cm) from the top of the purse, as shown right.

7 Fold over the flap, mark the position of the clasp, then apply the second part. You could cover the prongs on the inside with a scrap of grey felt if you wish.

Miss Messenger Bag

This casual cross-body bag is the perfect partner for the girl on the go. Spacious enough for travel documents and reading matter, it keeps your hands free as you do a bit of shopping in the airport. I have fused the fleece to the lining fabric this time, to reduce bulk and make the zip insertion on the outer bag neater.

Finished size

With flap open, 12½ x 15in (31.75 x 38cm)
With flap folded over, 12½ x 10½in (31.75 x 26.75cm), not including strap

What you need

36 x 18in (91.5 x 45.75cm) outer fabric
40 x 9in (101.5 x 23cm) faux leather
26 x 18in (66 x 45.75cm) lining fabric
26 x 18in (66 x 45.75cm) fusible fleece
Two 1in (2.5cm) D-rings
Two 1in (2.5cm) swivel snap hooks
10in (25.5cm) nylon zip
6in (15.25cm) of ¼in (5mm) wide ribbon to trim the zip pull
Magnetic clasp
Fabric glue pen

Cut

Two pieces of outer fabric measuring 13in (33cm) square

Two pieces of faux leather measuring 13 x 5in (33 x 13cm)

For the lining, two pieces of lining fabric and two pieces of fusible fleece measuring 13 x 18in (33 x 45.75cm)

For the pocket, two pieces of outer fabric measuring 10 x 8in (25.5 x 20.5cm)

For the strap, one piece of faux leather measuring 4 x 40in (10 x 101.5cm)

For the handles, two pieces of outer fabric measuring 4 x 11in (10 x 28cm)

For the tabs, two pieces of outer fabric measuring 2 x 3in (5 x 7.5cm)

1 Sew a piece of faux leather to the bottom of each of the outer fabric pieces. Press the seam open and top-stitch along each side of the seam. You will need to put a cloth over the seam when pressing so as not to melt the coating on the faux leather.

2 Take one of the pocket pieces and on the back, draw a box measuring 8 x ½in (20.5 x 1cm), centrally, 1½in (4cm) from the top. Draw a line straight through the centre of the box, and create a 'Y' shape at each end.

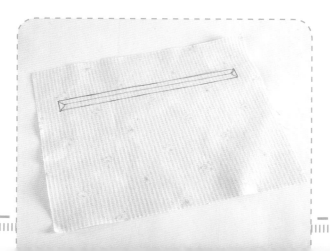

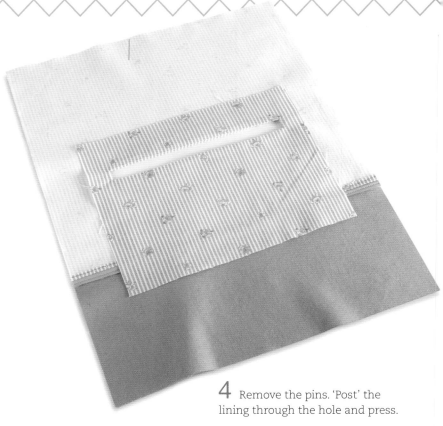

3 Pin the pocket right sides together with one side of the bag, centrally, 5½in (14cm) from the top. With a small stitch on your sewing machine, sew around the outside of the box. Using a sharp pair of scissors, cut along the centre line and the 'Y' shapes into the corners of the box (see page 22).

4 Remove the pins. 'Post' the lining through the hole and press.

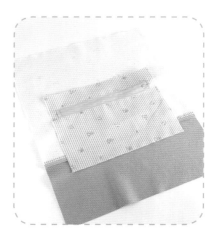

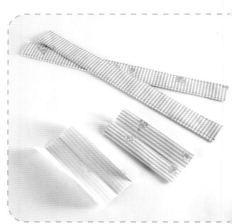

5 Apply glue around the pocket side of the zip opening. Place the zip slider-side down over the opening, making sure the coil of the zip is central and straight. (You could tack/baste by hand if you prefer). Sew around the zip using the zipper foot on your sewing machine; move the zip slider out of the way as you sew. Trim the ends of the zip if necessary.

6 Pin the remaining pocket fabric piece right sides together with the zip section – be careful not to pin through the main bag fabric. Sew the two pocket pieces together, keeping the main bag fabric out of the way, then remove the pins. Thread the ribbon through the zip pull and knot.

7 To make the handles and tabs, treat them all the same: fold the fabric pieces in half lengthways and crease. Fold the long sides to the centre and press, then fold in half and press (see page 17). Top-stitch along the two long sides of each strip.

8 Tack/baste the handles, facing downwards, to the top of the outer bag pieces, 4½in (11.5cm) from each side. Thread each tab through a D-ring, then tack/baste, facing inwards on each side of the bag, just above the zip, so that the tabs extend the side of the bag by 1in (2.5cm), then trim them back.

9 Fuse the fleece to the wrong side of the lining fabric pieces. Place one outer panel over the lining and trim if necessary so they are the same size. Fit one half of the magnetic clasp to the top of each lining piece, centrally, 1½in (4cm) from the top (see page 19).

Tip

I find the tabs easier to sew if they are cut longer than needed; trim the excess fabric away after tacking/basting.

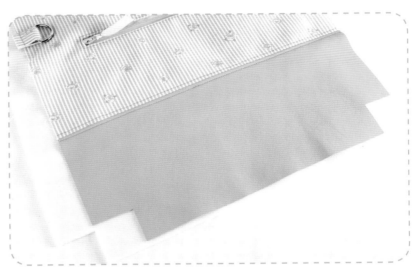

10 Cut a 1½in (4cm) square from the bottom corners of the outer and lining pieces.

11 Sew the outer pieces right sides together leaving the top and the cut-out corners unsewn; sew the lining pieces together in the same way, but also leave a 5in (13cm) turning gap in the base. Pull open the four corners so that the side and base seams meet, then sew straight across to make the base of each piece square.

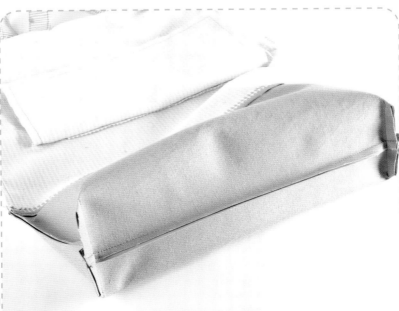

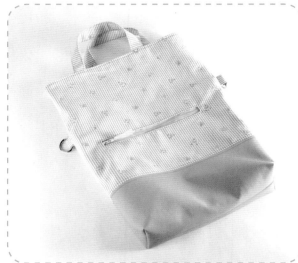

12 Turn the lining right side out. Drop the lining inside the outer bag with right sides together and sew around the top. Turn right side out and press, then sew the turning gap closed.

13 Push the lining inside the bag then top-stitch around the top.

14 For the strap, take the long strip of faux leather and fold the long edges to the centre. Clip or pin. Fold the fabric in half with the raw edges on the outside, sew across the short end and snip the corners. Repeat with the opposite end.

15 Fold the strip so that the raw edges are now on the inside, then sew along both sides. Thread each end through a swivel snap hook and sew to secure.

16 Clip the strap onto the D-rings at the sides of the bag and you're ready to go!

Tip

When sewing through thick fabrics, a denim needle will help. Try using a non-stick foot with faux leather or laminated fabric to reduce friction.

Mini Miss Messenger

This pretty purse is large enough to double as a stylish cosmetic bag.

Finished size

8½ x 6½in (21.5 x 16.5cm)

What you need

18 x 18in (46 x 46cm) outer fabric

13 x 18in (33 x 46cm) lining fabric

9in (23cm) square faux leather

13 x 18in (33 x 46cm) fusible fleece

6in (15.25cm) zip

Magnetic clasp

One swivel snap hook on a 1in (2.5cm) ring

6in (15.25cm) of ¼in (5mm) wide ribbon to decorate the zip pull

8in (20.5cm) of ¼in (5mm) wide ribbon for the bow and one button (optional)

Cut

Two pieces of outer fabric measuring 7 x 5in (18 x 13cm)

Two pieces of faux leather measuring 9 x 4½in (23 x 11cm)

Two pieces of lining fabric measuring 9 x 13in (23 x 33cm)

Two pieces of fusible fleece measuring 9 x 13in (23 x 33cm)

For the wristlet, one strip of outer fabric measuring 3 x 14in (7.5 x 35.5cm)

For the tab, one piece of outer fabric measuring 3 x 3in (7.5 x 7.5cm)

1 Sew the faux-leather strips to the bottom of the two larger outer pieces. Press the seam open and top-stitch either side. Place a cloth over the faux leather to avoid melting it with your iron.

2 Draw a box measuring 5 x ½in (13 x 1cm) on the wrong side of one of the pocket pieces, centrally, 1in (2.5cm) from the top, with a line across the centre forming a 'Y' shape at each end. Pin this piece right sides together with one outer bag piece 6in (15.25cm) from the top and sew around the box. Cut along the centre line and into the corners of the sewn box.

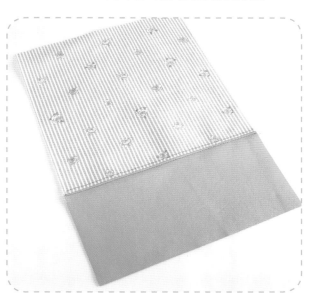

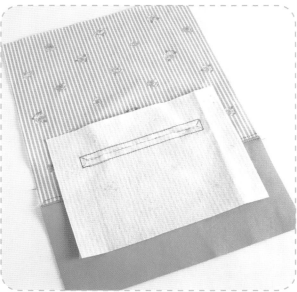

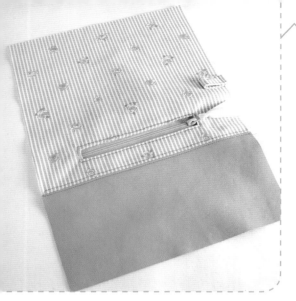

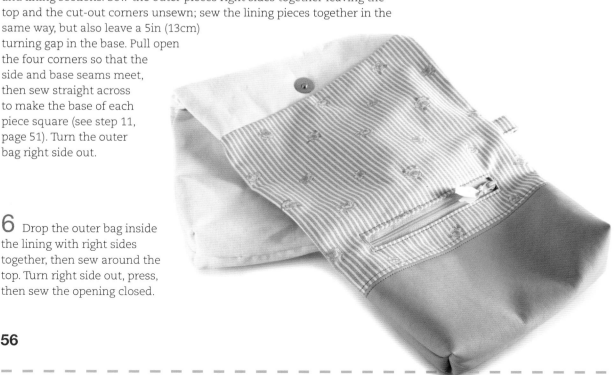

3 Push the pocket fabric through the hole and press. Fit the zip behind the hole and top-stitch in place (see step 5, page 50). Sew the second pocket piece right sides together to the first (see step 6, page 50), keeping the main bag fabric out of the way. Tie the ribbon to the zip pull. To make the tab, fold the fabric piece in half lengthways and crease. Fold the long sides to the centre and press, then fold in half again and press. Top-stitch along the two long sides. Fold it in half. Tack/baste the tab, facing inwards, along one side of the front of the bag, 5½in (14cm) from the top, and form a loop measuring 1in (2.5cm). Trim away any excess tab fabric.

4 Fuse the fleece to the wrong sides of the lining fabric. Apply the magnetic clasp to each side of the lining, centrally, 1in (2.5cm) from the top.

5 Cut a 1in (2.5cm) square from the bottom corners of both the outer and lining sections. Sew the outer pieces right sides together leaving the top and the cut-out corners unsewn; sew the lining pieces together in the same way, but also leave a 5in (13cm) turning gap in the base. Pull open the four corners so that the side and base seams meet, then sew straight across to make the base of each piece square (see step 11, page 51). Turn the outer bag right side out.

6 Drop the outer bag inside the lining with right sides together, then sew around the top. Turn right side out, press, then sew the opening closed.

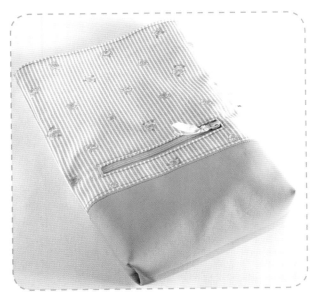

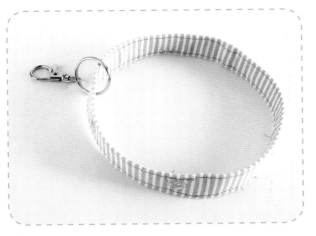

7 Push the lining inside the bag and top-stitch around the top. You may need to use your zipper foot to avoid sewing over the magnetic clasp.

8 For the wristlet, fold the fabric in half lengthways and press. Fold each long side to the centre, fold in half and press again. Open out the fabric, thread on the swivel snap hook, and sew the two short ends right sides together to make a loop. Fold the raw edges to the centre along the crease marks, then in half again, then top-stitch around both edges.

9 Sew across the loop just above the swivel snap to secure it, then attach to the tab on the side of the purse. Sew a bow and button to the flap to decorate.

Working Girl Tote

This is a good-sized, stylish tote for the working girl, large enough for paperwork and secure with the zipped panel in the lining. I've used quite a heavy wool fabric here; a lighter-weight cotton would give a completely different look. Allow a little extra fabric if you want to pattern match.

Tip
Make the tote up in bright fun colours for a fun beach bag!

Finished size

14½ x 12½ x 5½in (37 x 31.75 x 14cm), not including handles

What you need

54 x 18in (137 x 45.75cm) outer fabric

54 x 18in (137 x 45.75cm) lining fabric

45 x 18in (112 x 45.75cm) fusible fleece

15 x 5in (38 x 13cm) mesh bag base

Four bag feet

90in (228.5cm) piping: mine was shop-bought; to make your own see page 16

50in (127cm) of 1in (2.5cm) wide bias binding

20in (51cm) nylon zip

2½in (6.5cm) and 4in (10cm) circle templates

Strong wet fabric glue

Cut

Two pieces of outer fabric and fusible fleece measuring 14 x 11½in (35.5 x 29.25cm) for the front and back panels

Two pieces of lining measuring 14 x 12½in (35.5 x 31.75cm) for the front and back panels

One piece each of outer fabric, lining and fusible fleece measuring 14 x 6in (35.5 x 15.25cm) for the base

Two pieces of outer fabric, lining and fusible fleece measuring 11½ x 8in (29.25 x 20.5cm) for the ends: measure 1in (2.5cm) from each bottom corner, and cut from here to the top corners to taper

Two pieces each of outer fabric, lining and fusible fleece measuring 4 x 11in (10 x 28cm) for the zip panel

Two pieces of outer fabric measuring 1½ x 3in (4 x 7.5cm) for the zip tabs

One outer and one lining fabric piece, each measuring 6 x 7in (15.25 x 18cm) for the patch pocket

Two outer and two lining strips of fabric for the handles, each measuring 2½ x 20in (6.5 x 51cm)

1 Fuse the fleece to the back of the outer front and back panels. Curve the bottom two corners of the outer and lining front and back pieces using your 4in (10cm) circle template. Sew a piece of piping, raw edges together, around the sides and bottom of the front and back pieces, starting and stopping 1½in (4cm) from the top. Turn the ends of the piping to the outside of the edge to make neat.

2 Sew a strip of piping across the top of the outer pocket piece.

3 Sew the pocket lining to the outer pocket, right sides together, leaving a turning gap of about 3in (7.5cm) in one side. Turn right side out and press.

4 Sew the pocket to the front of the bag around the sides and bottom. You can see here how I've matched the pattern; this looks effective, but isn't so important on fabric with a smaller pattern.

5 Fuse the fleece to the wrong side of the outer end and base panels, then sew them together in a row, right sides facing, with the base panel in the middle.

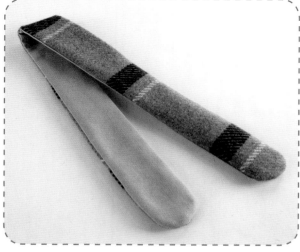

6 To make the handles, use your 2½in (6.5cm) circle template to round off each end of the outer and lining strips.

7 Sew each outer strip to a lining strip right sides together, leaving a turning gap of about 4in (10cm) in one side. Snip around the curves with pinking shears, turn right side out and press.

8 Fold each handle in half lengthways with the lining on the inside, and top-stitch the edges together 2in (5cm) from each end, as shown.

9 Open out the round ends of each handle, spread a little wet glue on the back and pin to the top of the bag front and back, 4in (10cm) from either side and 3in (7.5cm) from the top. When the glue is dry, remove the pins and sew in place. (I find it easier to glue first so that the handles don't move as I try to sew around the pins.)

10 Sew the base and end panels to the front and back of the bag, right sides together. Start by folding all pieces in half to crease the centre, match the centre base to the bottom centre front and back of the bag and pin. You may need to trim a little fabric from the top of the bag. As there is no pattern for this bag, your curved corners may be slightly different to mine, which could affect the sides and end pieces matching up – this is not a problem, simply trim them to size when sewn.

11 Measure the base of the bag inside the seams and then cut a piece of bag base to this size. Glue to the inside bottom of the bag, then apply the bag feet to each outer corner of the base, 1in (2.5cm) from each side.

12 To make the zipped panel, take each outer and lining zip panel piece, fold the short ends over by ¼in (5mm) and press; secure in place with pins. With the zipper foot on your machine, sew the zip, facing downwards, centrally to the right side of one outer piece.

13 Repeat with the opposite outer piece, then add the linings to the remaining sides of the zip. Make sure the folded ends of the panel line up, then top-stitch around each panel, along the two short ends and zip edge.

14 Trim the zip so that the ends extend the panel by 3in (7.5cm). Take a zip tab piece, fold the short ends over wrong sides together and press. Fold the tab in half right sides together and sew around the three raw edges to make a small pouch. Repeat.

15 Turn right side out and press, then slip one tab over each end of the zip and sew in a box. You might want to sew the open ends of the zip together by hand beforehand to stop them slipping, or you could use a spot of wet glue to secure before sewing.

16 Take the two front and back lining pieces and cut a 3in (7.5cm) strip from the top of each side.

17 Sew the zipped panel, zip facing upwards, to the top of the lower section of one side of the lining, then sew the upper section over the top, right sides facing, sandwiching the zip panel in the centre.

18 Sew the second side of the lining to the opposite side of the zip panel in the same way. Sew the lining end and base pieces together in the same way as you did the outer fabric pieces. Mark the centre base positions, pin, then sew to the lining panels.

19 When you sew on the second panel you will have a complete lining section with the zipped panel sitting near the top.

20 Drop the lining inside the bag and tack/baste the two sections together around the top. Apply bias tape around the top of the bag to finish (see page 18).

Working Girl Wallet

This is quite a large purse with both open and zipped pockets, so it would also make a useful travel bag for jewellery or make-up.

1 Take the large outer, lining and wadding/batting pieces and, using your circle template and marker, cut a curve from the top of each piece.

2 Sew the zips, slider side down, to each short end of one of the pocket lining pieces.

Finished size

Closed: 9 x 6in (23 x 15.25cm)
Open: 9 x 16in (23 x 41cm)

What you need

18 x 16in (46 x 41cm) outer fabric

38 x 15½in (97 x 40cm) lining fabric

Two 8in (20.5cm) nylon zips

Magnetic clasp

9 x 16in (23 x 41cm) wadding/batting

82in (210cm) of 1in (2.5cm) wide bias binding

12in (30.5cm) of ¼in (5mm) wide ribbon to trim the zips

9in (23cm) circle template and marking pen

Cut

One piece each of outer fabric, lining and wadding/batting measuring 9 x 16in (23 x 41cm)

Four lining pieces measuring 7½ x 11in (19 x 28cm) for the zipped pockets

One piece each of outer fabric and lining for the card pockets measuring 9 x 6½in (23 x 16.5cm)

For the handle, one piece of outer fabric measuring 8 x 2in (20.5 x 5cm)

3 Sew a second lining piece over the top so that the zip is sandwiched in between the two lining pieces. Turn right side out.

4 Sew the other two pieces of lining to the opposite side of the zip in the same way to make a tube. Sew the raw edges together, leaving a turning gap in one side of about 3in (7.5cm).

5 Turn right side out, then sew the opening closed. Press.

6 On the long lining piece, measure and mark a line 6in (15.25cm) from the bottom, then 5½in (14cm) above this line.

7 For the card pockets, place the outer and lining pieces wrong sides together, and apply bias binding to each 9in (23cm) side (see page 18).

8 Measure and mark halfway across the pocket in both directions. Place the pocket over the 6in (15.25cm) line on the lining and sew, then sew across the pockets to divide into four sections.

Tip

If your lining fabric isn't too thick, it would be easy to add another zipped pocket to the centre of the purse; cut the fabric 1in (2.5cm) shorter so that the zips don't sit on top of each other and create too much bulk.

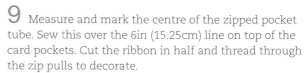

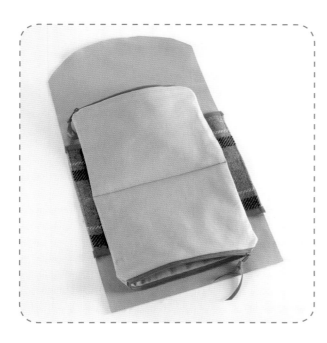

9 Measure and mark the centre of the zipped pocket tube. Sew this over the 6in (15.25cm) line on top of the card pockets. Cut the ribbon in half and thread through the zip pulls to decorate.

10 To make the handle, fold the two short edges of the fabric under by ¼in (5mm) and press. Fold the two long sides to the centre, wrong sides together, and press. Fold an 8in (20.5cm) length of bias binding in half and press, then top-stitch along the handle to cover the raw edges.

11 Sew the handle to the outer fabric, 1½in (4cm) from each side and 4in (10cm) from the curved top. I've sewn my handle on by hand as I wanted the stitches to be invisible; sew in a box shape by machine if you wish.

12 Apply one half of the magnetic clasp to the lining, centrally, 1in (2.5cm) from the curved top, and the second half of the clasp to the outer fabric, centrally, 2½in (6.5cm) from the straight bottom side.

13 Place the outer and lining sections wrong sides together and tack/baste around the edge, then apply bias binding all the way round.

14 Fold the flap over the purse to close.

First Class Caddy

Slip the strap on the back of this briefcase-style bag over the handles of your suitcase or trolley to keep it secure as you walk; the zipped pocket is the perfect place to keep tickets and passports safe.

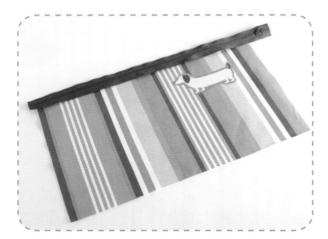

1 Sew the 17in (43cm) zip, sliders face down onto the top edge of the pocket, to the right-hand side. You'll see that the zip is too long: I find it easier to sew with the sliders moved out of the way, then trim the zip to size later.

2 As the print on my dog fabric is so large I thought it would be fun to cut out one of the shapes and appliqué it on to the pocket of my bag. I've used a satin stitch on my sewing machine.

Finished size

14½ x 10½ x 2½in (37 x 26.75 x 6.5cm)

What you need

30 x 11in (76 x 28cm) dog fabric, plus optional extra for appliqué

31 x 15in (78.75 x 38cm) striped fabric

41 x 18in (104 x 46cm) lining fabric

30 x 11in (76 x 28cm) medium-weight fusible stabilizer

46in (117cm) of 1in (2.5cm) wide webbing

17in (43cm) nylon zip: I used a continuous zip and added two sliders that meet

28in (71cm) nylon zip

Two 1in (2.5cm) D-rings

Two 1in (2.5cm) swivel snaps

One 1in (2.5cm) slider

14½ x 2½in (37 x 6.5cm) mesh bag base

Strong wet fabric glue

Cut

Two pieces of dog fabric measuring 15 x 11in (38 x 28cm) for the front and back

Two pieces of lining measuring 15 x 11in (38 x 28cm) for the front and back

Two pieces of fusible stabilizer measuring 15 x 11in (38 x 28cm) for the front and back

One piece of striped fabric for the pocket, measuring 15 x 7in (38 x 18cm)

One piece of lining for the pocket measuring 15 x 7in (38 x 18cm)

One piece of striped fabric measuring 15 x 3in (38 x 7.5cm) for the base

One piece of lining measuring 15 x 3in (38 x 7.5cm) for the base

Two pieces of striped fabric for the zip panel measuring 26 x 2in (66 x 5cm)

Two pieces of lining for the zip panel measuring 26 x 2in (66 x 5cm)

Two pieces of striped fabric for the end of zip panel measuring 3 x 7in (7.5 x 18cm)

Two pieces of lining for the end of zip panel measuring 3 x 7in (7.5 x 18cm)

Two pieces of striped fabric measuring 8½ x 4½in (21.5 x 11.5cm) for the rear strap

Two 1½in (4cm) pieces of webbing

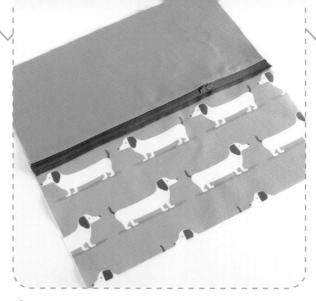

3 Sew the top of the pocket lining to the opposite side of the zip. Press, then top-stitch along the side of the zip. Trim the zip to the size of the pocket.

4 Measure and mark a line 4in (10cm) down from the top of the front bag panel. Place this piece and the pocket right sides together with the zip over the marked line (with the bottom of the pocket at the top of the outer fabric, as shown); sew along the zip tape.

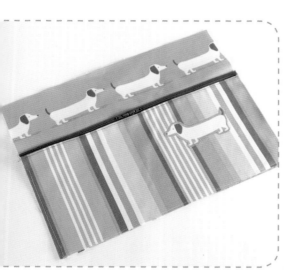

5 Fold down the pocket and tack/baste around the sides and bottom.

6 Make up the rear strap by sewing the two fabric pieces right sides together, leaving a turning gap in one seam of about 3in (7.5cm). Snip off the corners and turn right side out. Press. Top-stitch along the top and bottom.

7 Fuse the stabilizer to the wrong side of the dog-print fabric pieces. Pin the rear strap to the centre back of the bag, lifting the strap so that it doesn't lie flat, as shown. Sew along the two short edges, removing the pins as you sew.

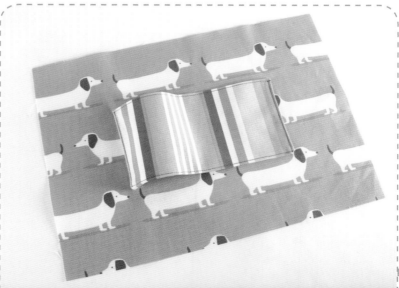

8 To make the zip panel, sew the two stripe fabric pieces right sides together with the 28in (71cm) zip. Sew the lining pieces to the opposite side, sandwiching the zip in between the two fabric pieces. Press the fabric away from the zip, then top-stitch either side. Trim the ends of the zip.

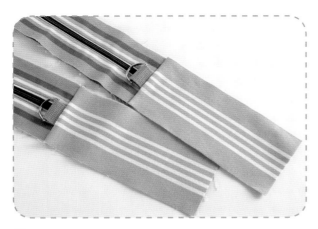

9 Take the two 1½in (4cm) lengths of webbing, thread each through a D-ring and sew facing inwards over each end of the zip. Sew the two striped zip panel ends right sides together to the ends of the zip panel, then sew the lining pieces to the opposite sides. Open out and press.

10 Fold the zip panel in half and crease the centre mark. Fold the front bag panel in half and crease the centre top. Pin, then sew the zip panel right sides together to the front of the bag, matching the two centre crease marks. The zip panel will be a little longer than the side panel. Remove the pins.

11 Sew the back of the bag to the zip panel in the same way. Trim away any excess from the zipped panel. Pin, then sew in the base of the bag, again, right sides together.

12 Start with the bag right side out and the zip open. Pin the front lining piece right sides together to the front of the bag, by turning the bag and trapping the whole of the back of the bag and zip panel between the two pieces. Sew around the top and sides, leaving the bottom open. Turn right side out and you'll have a really neat seam with no raw edges showing. Repeat to attach the remaining lining to the back of the bag. Turn right side out.

13 Wrap the base lining fabric around the mesh bag base, fold the ends inwards and tack/baste.

14 Drizzle a little wet glue around the edge of the seam side of the base, then push inside the bag, being careful not to get glue onto the lining. The bottom seams should tuck under the bag base. If you prefer you could tack/baste this in place by hand when the glue is dry.

15 Take the remaining webbing; thread one end through the centre of the slider and sew. Take the opposite end through a swivel snap, back over the centre of the slider then through the second swivel snap and sew.

16 Attach the straps to the D-rings.

17 Slip the rear strap over the handles of your suitcase. Bon voyage!

Tip
Unclip the strap and thread it through the handle of your suitcase for extra security.

First Class Passport Wallet

Passport? Check. Tickets? Check. Credit Cards? Check. Keep all of your travel essentials to hand in this useful wallet! I've just used interfacing on the outer fabric this time to reduce bulk in the pockets. If your fabric is quite fine, a lightweight cotton interfacing will still give the pockets a bit of structure.

Finished size

9½ x 4¾in (24 x 12cm)

What you need

25 x 15in (63.5 x 38cm) outer fabric
10 x 30in (25.5 x 76.25cm) lining fabric
10in (25.5cm) square medium-weight fusible interfacing
Magnetic clasp
6in (15.25cm) and 4in (10cm) circle templates

Cut

One piece of outer fabric measuring 10in (25.5cm) square
One piece of lining fabric measuring 10in (25.5cm) square
Two pieces of outer fabric for the passport pocket, measuring 4½ x 6in (11.5 x 15.25cm)
Four pieces of lining fabric for the ticket pockets measuring 10 x 4½in (25.5 x 11.5cm)
Two pieces of outer fabric for the card pockets measuring 10 x 3in (25.5 x 7.5cm)
Two pieces of outer fabric for the passport pocket flap measuring 4 x 3in (10 x 7.5cm)
Two pieces of outer fabric for the wallet flap measuring 4 x 9in (10 x 23cm)

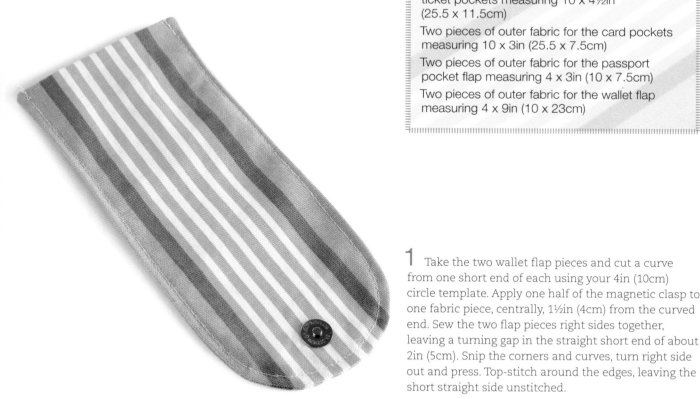

1 Take the two wallet flap pieces and cut a curve from one short end of each using your 4in (10cm) circle template. Apply one half of the magnetic clasp to one fabric piece, centrally, 1½in (4cm) from the curved end. Sew the two flap pieces right sides together, leaving a turning gap in the straight short end of about 2in (5cm). Snip the corners and curves, turn right side out and press. Top-stitch around the edges, leaving the short straight side unstitched.

2 Fuse the interfacing to the wrong side of the 10in (25.5cm) square of outer fabric. Measure and mark 3in (7.5cm) in from the right-hand edge, 5in (12.75cm) down from the top. Apply the second half of the magnetic snap at this point. Sew the straight end of the wallet flap to the back, centrally, 3in (7.5cm) from the left-hand edge, in a ½in (1cm) wide box shape to make it secure.

3 Place the two passport pocket pieces right sides together and, using your 6in (15.25cm) circle template, mark then cut a curve from the top left-hand corner. Sew the two pieces right sides together just around the curve, snip into the seam allowance then turn right side out and press. Top-stitch around the seam.

4 Pin this piece to the right side of one of the ticket pocket pieces, then tack/baste along the sides of the pocket; remove the pins.

5 Take the passport pocket flap pieces and place them right sides together. Cut a curve on the bottom left-hand corner using your 6in (15.25cm) circle template. Sew the two pieces right sides together, leaving a turning gap of about 2in (5cm) in the top. Snip into the curved seam, turn right side out and press. Top-stitch around the curved and short straight sides.

6 Place the flap centrally over the top of the passport pocket, leaving a ¾in (2cm) gap, and sew across the top. This little flap is important – it will stop your passport slipping out!

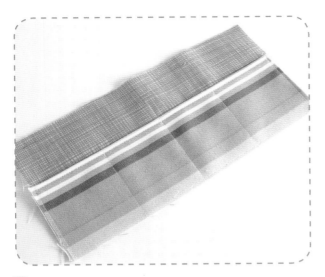

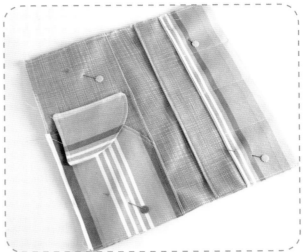

7 Sew the two card pocket pieces right sides together across the long top edge, turn right side out and press. Top-stitch along the seam. Pin to one of the ticket pocket pieces, with the raw edges aligned. Measure and mark a line along the centre of the ticket pocket, then 2¼in (5.75cm) either side. Sew along these lines to divide the pocket into four.

8 Place the remaining ticket pocket pieces right sides together with the card pocket and passport pockets. Sew across the long top edges, making sure you don't sew the passport pocket flap into the seam! Turn to the right side and press, then top-stitch along the seams. Pin the pockets to each side of the 10in (25.5cm) square lining piece, then tack/baste around the edge.

9 Pin the outer section of the wallet to the lining, right sides facing, tucking the flap out of the way so you don't sew over it. Make sure that the flap on the outer section is sitting at right angles to the pockets so that the pockets are kept flat when the wallet is folded. Sew all the way around, leaving a turning gap of about 4in (10cm) in one side. Remove the pins, snip across the corners, turn right side out and press. Top-stitch all the way round to finish.

Tip

Add a loop of tape to the side of the wallet before sewing up in step 9 so that you can clip a chain onto it, then another inside your travel bag to keep your wallet really secure.

77

Ladies' Day Bag

I really like the contrasting textures of cotton, lace and faux leather in this bag, and keeping the colours tonal gives a classy appearance. I've used a firm, leather-like interfacing to give my bag structure; if you're new to sewing, you may find fusible fleece a little easier to manage, although your bag will have a softer finish. I've left the inside plain on this bag, but you could easily add a zipped pocket if you wanted (see pages 22–23).

Finished size

15 x 11 x 2½in (38 x 28 x 6.5cm), not including strap

What you need

32 x 12in (82 x 30.5cm) lace-covered fabric

32 x 12in (82 x 30.5cm) lining fabric

32 x 12in (82 x 30.5cm) firm single-sided fusible interfacing

24 x 16in (61 x 41cm) faux leather

12 x 8in (30.5 x 20.5cm) fusible fleece

Purse tongue lock

Two 1in (2.5cm) rectangular rings

1in (2.5cm) rectangular slider

3in (7.5cm) and 7in (18cm) circle templates

Strong wet fabric glue

Repositionable spray fabric adhesive

Fabric clips

1 Cut two pieces of outer (lace) fabric measuring 16 x 12in (41 x 30.5cm). Round off the two bottom corners using your 3in (7.5cm) template. Cut a 1in (2.5cm) 'V' shape from each curved corner, making sure they are in the same position on each side. These are your darts.

2 Measure and mark 1in (2.5cm) in from each side of the top of the fabric, and trim from here in a straight line to the curve, making the top of the bag narrower than the base.

Tip

Make your own lace-covered fabric by simply spraying the wrong side of a length of lace with repositionable spray fabric adhesive and placing it over a piece of plain fabric.

3 For the flap, cut two pieces of faux leather measuring 12 x 8in (30.5 x 20.5cm), making sure you leave a 24 x 8in (61 x 20.5cm) strip for the strap (see step 10). Mark the bottom centre point on one piece and, using your 7in (18cm) circle template, draw a curve. Draw two further curves either side of the central curve and cut. Fold the fabric in half to make sure the flap is symmetrical. Use this as a template to cut a second faux leather flap. Fuse fleece to the back of one of the pieces. Don't iron the faux leather from the right side as it will melt – instead, place a cloth over the fleece and iron from the wrong side.

4 Sew the two flap pieces right sides together leaving the top open. Snip into the curves and turn right side out. Top-stitch around the seam. Add the tongue side of the clasp to the centre front of the flap.

5 Fuse the firm interfacing to the wrong sides of the outer lace pieces, then use them as templates to cut two pieces of lining fabric. Tack/baste the flap right sides together to the top of the back of the bag.

6 Place the front and back sections of the bag wrong sides together, fold the flap over the front and mark the position of the clasp, measuring to make sure it is central. Fit the second part of the clasp to the front of the bag.

7 On the outer bag pieces, sew in each dart by folding the two halves of the cut-out triangles right sides together, and curve your stitch line gently as you sew.

8 Sew the two outer pieces of the bag right sides together around the sides and bottom. Trim the interfacing back to the seam, then turn right side out. (The fabric is quite thick now so will crease, but the creases will disappear when ironed.)

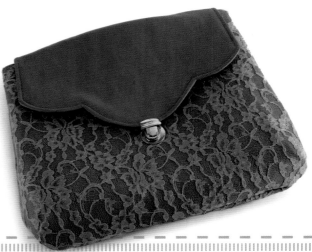

9 Sew the two lining pieces together in the same way: sew the darts, then sew the pieces right sides together, this time leaving a turning gap of about 7in (18cm) in the base.

10 To make the strap, you will need a length of faux leather measuring 36 x 4in (91.5 x 10cm) – I joined two strips together. Fold each short end inwards by ½in (1cm) – a little repositionable spray helps here. Fold the two long edges to the centre, then fold the strap in half again. Top-stitch all the way round. Thread one end through the centre of the slider and sew in a box shape.

11 Cut two pieces of faux leather, each measuring 4 x 6in (10 x 15.25cm). Fold the long sides to the centre, then fold in half again and top-stitch along the sides. Thread each piece through a rectangular ring. Fold one short side under by ½in (1cm). Put a spot of glue onto the remaining end, fold the whole loop flat and secure with a clip until the glue is dry.

12 Sew these tabs to each side of the bag, over the seam, with the top of the faux leather meeting the top of the bag. You may find it easier to take the accessory compartment off your sewing machine, and sew in straight lines instead of a box shape, as the stiff fabric may be difficult to manipulate under the needle.

81

13 Drop the outer bag inside the lining, with right sides together. Sew around the top. Trim the interfacing back to the seam. Turn right side out through the gap in the lining, then sew the opening closed.

14 Push the lining inside the bag, then carefully top-stitch around the top. Attach the strap to the bag by threading it through one of the rectangular rings, back through the slider then through the second rectangular ring. Make sure the strap isn't twisted, then sew the end to the strap to secure.

15 One final press and you're finished!

Ladies' Day Purse

Here's a simple way to design your own purse using a rectangular clasp. I've used lace to match my bag, but it would look just as good in denim, faux leather or printed cotton. Once you've made the template for the top of the purse, you can make the belly of the purse in any shape or size you like!

Finished size

8 x 6in (20.5 x 15.25cm)

What you need

6in (15.25cm) rectangle clasp frame

10 x 14in (25.5 x 35.5cm) outer fabric

10 x 14in (25.5 x 35.5cm) lining fabric

10 x 14in (25.5 x 35.5cm) fusible fleece

Strong wet fabric glue

Paper, ruler and pen to make a pattern

Tweezers

1 Place the purse frame onto the paper and draw around the outside of the frame from one hinge to the other. Draw a 3in (7.5cm) line at an angle from the top right-hand corner to 1in (2.5cm) away from the hinge. Measure the centre of the frame, then draw a 6in (15.25cm) line, which indicates the depth of the purse. Draw 5in (13cm) from the bottom centre to the right-hand side, then join up the side.

2 Fold your pattern in half to make symmetrical, and cut out the shape.

3 Fuse the fleece to the wrong side of the outer fabric pieces. From your template cut two pieces from outer fabric and two pieces from lining fabric.

4 Measure and mark 3in (7.5cm) down from the top, along the side of the lining pieces. Place each lining piece right sides together with an outer piece, and sew around the top between the two markings.

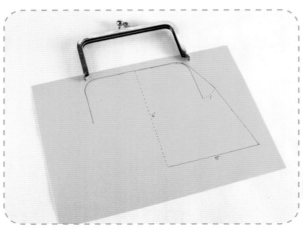

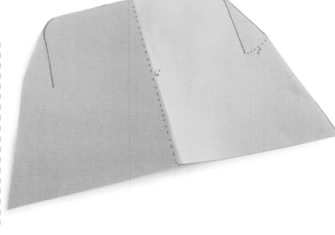

5 Open out the two pieces and place them so that the outer fabrics and the linings are right sides together. Sew around the outer pieces, starting and stopping at the existing stitch line. Flip the fabric over and repeat with the lining, but this time leave a turning gap of about 3in (7.5cm) in the base.

6 Turn right side out, sew the turning gap closed and push the lining inside the purse. Press. Drizzle a little wet glue inside one side of the frame. Push one side of the top of the purse into the frame – tweezers will really help here. While the glue is still wet, manoeuvre the fabric so that it sits centrally in the frame.

7 When the glue is completely dry, repeat with the second side of the frame.

VIDEO
Fitting a purse frame

Tip
Make your purse pretty by adding buttons or bows as decorations!

85

Cocktail Hour Bag

Accessorize for a girl's night out with this beautiful bag! The chain strap gives it a dressy look, but you could make a fabric strap if you prefer.

Finished size

12 x 9 x 2¾in (30.5 x 23 x 7cm)

What you need

11 x 8in (28 x 20.5cm) floral fabric

23½ x 18in (59.75 x 46cm) lining fabric

23½ x 18in (59.75 x 46cm) firm single-sided fusible interfacing

25 x 9in (63.5 x 23cm) spotted outer fabric

Twist lock

Two ½in (1cm) eyelets

Chain strap of your chosen length

Erasable ink pen and ruler

Cut

One piece of floral fabric measuring 11 x 8in (28 x 20.5cm)

One piece of lining fabric measuring 11 x 8in (28 x 20.5cm)

One piece of interfacing measuring 11 x 8in (28 x 20.5cm)

Two pieces of spotted fabric measuring 12½ x 9in (31.75 x 23cm)

Two pieces of lining measuring 12½ x 9in (31.75 x 23cm)

Two pieces of interfacing measuring 12½ x 9in (31.75 x 23cm)

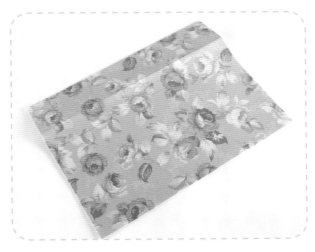

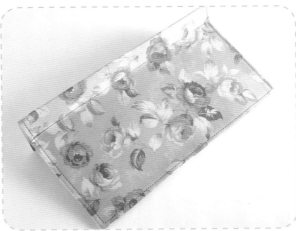

1 Fuse the interfacing to the wrong sides of the floral and spotted fabrics. Measure and mark 2in (5cm) and 3in (7.5cm) down from the top of the floral fabric and draw a line across the width of the fabric at each point.

2 Sew the matching-sized lining right sizes together with the floral fabric piece, leaving the top edge open. Snip off the corners and turn right side out. Finger press the seams (using heat may remove your markings if you've used a heat-erasable pen, although it's not a problem – you can simply re draw them) then top-stitch around the sewn sides. Fold the piece lining sides together at the first drawn line, then sew along the second line through all layers.

3 Mark the position of the twist lock, centrally, 1¾in (4.5cm) up from the edge of the flap.

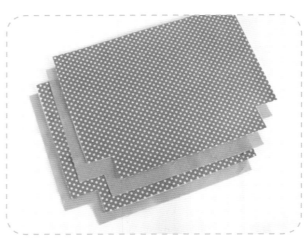

4 Cut out the hole and around the screw holes with a quick-unpick or small sharp scissors. Cut a small hole to start, then increase the size slightly in stages if needed, to make sure the finished hole isn't too big.

5 Fit the lock (see page 20). Apply the eyelets to the folded top of the flap, 2in (5cm) in from each side (refer to the manufacturer's instructions).

6 Take the spotted pieces and their corresponding lining pieces and cut a 1½in (4cm) square from the bottom corners of each.

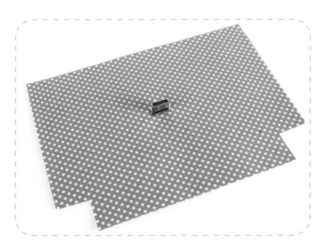

7 Fit the remaining half of the twist lock to the front of the bag, centrally, 2½in (6.5cm) down from the top.

8 Sew the flap centrally to the top of the bag back with right sides together.

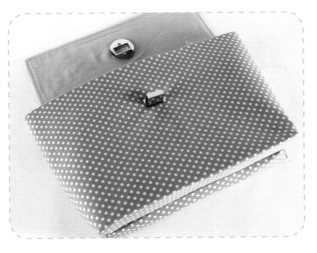

Tip

If you prefer a softer look to your bag, use fusible fleece instead of firm interfacing.

9 Sew the two outer bag pieces right sides together, leaving the top and cut-out corners unsewn. Squash the cut-out corners so that the side seams sit over the bottom seam and sew across to make the bag base square. Turn right side out.

10 Repeat with the lining pieces, but this time leave a turning gap of about 5in (13cm) in the base.

11 Drop the bag inside the lining, right sides together, and sew around the top using the free arm on your sewing machine.

12 Turn right side out, sew the turning gap closed then push the lining inside the bag. Press, then top-stitch around the top of the bag. Attach the chain to the eyelets.

Cocktail Hour Purse

This simple purse with zipped inside pocket is ideal to keep your coins and lipstick handy on a night out! I've used fusible fleece instead of the firm stabilizer I used with the matching bag, as I find it easier to work with on smaller projects.

1 Fuse the fleece to the wrong side of the large floral piece of fabric, and to the wrong side of the spotted front piece – the 8 x 5in (20.5 x 12.5cm) piece.

2 Mark the centre of the front spotted piece by folding in half and creasing, then apply the thicker part of the magnetic clasp 2½in (6.5cm) from the top. Fit the second half of the clasp to the centre top of the large spotted piece of fabric, 1in (2.5cm) down from the top.

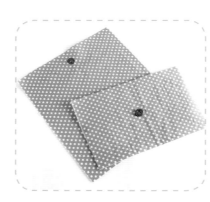

3 Sew the zip to the top of the pocket pieces, sandwiching the zip tape in between the spotted and floral pieces. Open out and press; top-stitch along each side of the zip. I like to use zips that are too long then trim them to size, as I can move the slider out of the way to give me a neater stitch line. Finally, trim the zip, making sure you've moved the slider to the centre. Fold the pocket in half, so the spotted lining pieces meet.

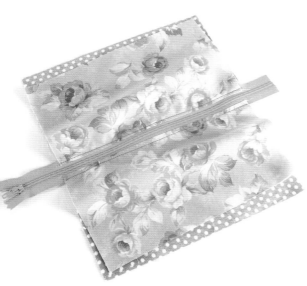

Finished size

7¼ x 5½in (18.5 x 14cm)

What you need

15 x 16in (38 x 41cm) floral fabric
15 x 16in (38 x 41cm) spotted fabric
8 x 15in (20.5 x 38cm) fusible fleece
Magnetic clasp
Two ¼in (5mm) eyelets
20in (51cm) chain strap
10in (25.5cm) zip
3in (7.5cm) square of green felt
4 x 1in (10 x 2.5cm) grey felt
Small wooden bead
Erasable ink pen and ruler
Strong wet fabric glue

Cut

One piece of floral fabric measuring 8 x 10in (20.5 x 25.5cm) for the back and flap
One piece of spotted fabric measuring 8 x 10in (20.5 x 25.5cm)
One piece of fusible fleece measuring 8 x 10in (20.5 x 25.5cm)
One piece of floral fabric measuring 8 x 5in (20.5 x 12.5cm) for the front
One piece of spotted fabric measuring 8 x 5in (20.5 x 12.5cm)
One piece of fusible fleece measuring 8 x 5in (20.5 x 12.5cm)
Two pieces of floral fabric measuring 8 x 4½in (20.5 x 11.5cm) for the zip pocket
Two pieces of spotted fabric measuring 8 x 4½in (20.5 x 11.5cm) for the zip pocket

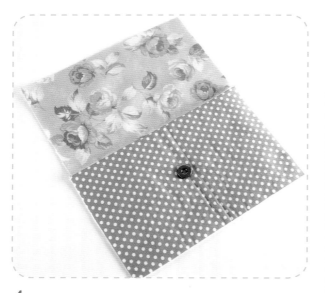

4 Sew the 8 x 5in (20.5 x 12.5cm) front floral fabric piece right sides together with the 8 x 5in (20.5 x 12.5cm) front spotted piece along the top edge only, then open out and press, as shown.

5 Fold the piece sewn in step 4 in half, wrong sides together and press, then top-stitch along the seam. Place this piece, spotted side down, over the bottom of the large floral piece. Place the folded and trimmed zipped pocket on top, then sew across the bottom.

6 Pin the remaining spotted fabric right sides together over the pocket and sew all the way round, leaving a turning gap of about 4in (10cm) in the base. Snip across the corners.

7 Remove the pins, turn right side out and sew up the turning gap; press. Fold over the flap, then draw a line ½in (1cm) from the fold with erasable ink. Sew along this line. Punch a small hole ½in (1cm) in from each top corner and fit the eyelets according to your manufacturer's instructions. Add the chain strap.

8 Cut out two felt leaves and one flower using the templates on page 128. Make a running stitch along the straight side of the flower and pull the thread to gather. Sew a bead to the centre, then glue to one side of the purse flap with the leaves underneath.

Tip

If you prefer a wristlet instead of the chain strap, cut a piece of fabric measuring 9 x 8½in (23 x 21.5cm), fold the long edges to the centre and press, then fold in half again and press. Open out the creases, thread the fabric through a swivel snap then sew the short ends of the fabric right sides together (making sure the fabric isn't twisted). Re-fold the crease lines then top-stitch along both sides. Place the swivel snap so that the seam sits within it, and sew straight across to secure it.

Crafty Girl's Folder Holder

The hardware on this bag makes it look satchel-like, and the slimline shape makes it a useful pouch for paperwork and stationery. If you have a particular folder in mind, measure the size of it and add 1in (2.5cm) to the width, then use this as the width measurement of your fabric.

Finished size

12½ x 9½in (31.75 x 24cm)

What you need

26 x 9½in (66 x 24cm) plain outer fabric

26 x 18in (66 x 46cm) lining fabric

26 x 9½in (66 x 24cm) fusible fleece

26 x 8in (66 x 20.5cm) patterned outer fabric

70in (180cm) of 1in (2.5cm) wide webbing

Two 1in (2.5cm) sliders

Two 1in (2.5cm) rectangular rings

Two 1in (2.5cm) metal caps (sometimes called zipper ends)

Four ³/₈in (1cm) Chicago screws and a hole punch

Erasable ink pen and ruler

Cut

Two pieces of plain outer fabric measuring 13 x 9½in (33 x 24cm)

Two pieces of fusible fleece measuring 13 x 9½in (33 x 24cm)

Two pieces of lining fabric measuring 13 x 10in (33 x 25.5cm)

Two pieces of patterned outer fabric measuring 13 x 8in (33 x 20.5cm) for the pockets

Two pieces of lining fabric measuring 13 x 8in (33 x 20.5cm) for the pockets

Two lengths of webbing each measuring 3in (7.5cm)

Two lengths of webbing each measuring 4in (10cm)

Cut the remaining webbing in half

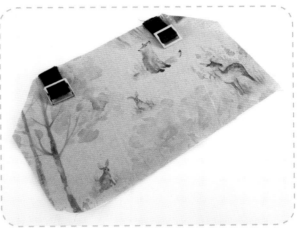

1 Take the outer and lining pocket pieces, measure and mark 2½in (6.5cm) from each top corner across the top and down the sides. Draw a diagonal line joining the marks and cut along it.

2 Take the 4in (10cm) lengths of webbing, thread through the centre of your sliders and sew, facing inwards, ½in (1cm) from each side of the top of one outer pocket piece.

3 Repeat with the 3in (7.5cm) strips of webbing and the remaining outer pocket piece, this time threading them through the rectangular rings.

4 Place each of the outer pocket pieces right sides together with a lining piece, then sew all round, leaving the bottom straight edge open. Turn right side out and press.

5 Fuse the fleece to the wrong sides of the plain outer fabric pieces. Sew the lining pieces right sides together to the outer fabric pieces along the top edge. Place each pocket over the bottom right side of the outer pieces and tack/baste in place. At this point you could stitch along the pocket to make dividing lines if you wish.

6 Pin both sections of the bag right sides together, matching lining to lining and outer to outer, then sew all the way around, leaving a turning gap of about 4in (10cm) in the bottom of the lining. Turn right side out and press. Sew the opening closed.

7 Push the lining inside the bag and press. You'll see that, as the lining is a little longer, a band of lining fabric overlaps the top of the bag. Thread each end of one of the webbing straps through the sliders, then add a metal cap to each end. Fix the strap by punching a hole and adding a Chicago screw through each end of the strap and into the pocket.

8 Take one end of the remaining strap, thread it through one of the rectangular rings and fix with a Chicago screw. Thread the opposite end of the strap through the second rectangular ring, measure this strap against the first to make sure the lengths are the same and then fix the second screw in place.

9 Crafting on the go!

Tip

The whole bag can be made without hardware if you wish: instead of sewing the webbing loops into the pockets, sew the ends of the webbing straps directly onto the pockets. I've added a contrast top-stitch and a couple of buttons to this one, made the pocket 1in (2.5cm) deeper, then divided it in two with a line of stitches down the centre. See how easy it is to adapt!

VIDEO
Crafty Girl's Purse

Crafty Girl's Purse

A crafty girl needs a pouch for pens and a notepad to write down ideas, somewhere to keep receipts, postage stamps and, of course, loose change for a well-deserved cuppa. This accordion purse fits the bill perfectly!

1 Fuse the fleece to the wrong side of the outer fabric. Draw an arc using your circle template around the end of the fabric that will form the flap, then cut. Use this piece as a template to cut the lining to the same shape.

2 Apply the slimmer section of the magnetic clasp centrally 1in (2.5cm) from the curved side of the lining, and the remaining section 1in (2.5cm) centrally from the straight bottom side of the outer fabric.

3 Trim the ends off the zip, making the zip 7in (18cm) long. Sandwich each end of the zip between two zip tab pieces that are right sides facing, aligning the raw ends with the ends of the zip. Sew across the ends of the zip with a ¼in (5mm) seam allowance, then finger press the fabric pieces back at each end. Top-stitch if you would like.

4 Place the zip right sides facing with one of the zip pocket pieces, aligning the edges, and sew.

5 Sew the second pocket piece over the top, sandwiching the zip in the centre – both lining pieces are attached to the same side of the zip. Trim the ends of the tabs away.

6 Fold the edges of the fabric over to either side of the second side of the zip and sew – you'll create two tubes joined together by the zip. Again, trim off the excess tab fabric. Push one tube inside the other so that the zip pull is on the outside and press.

7 To make the divider panels, fold each piece of fabric in half (8½ x 4½/21.5 x 11.5cm), right sides together, and sew across the open edge to make a tube.

8 Turn both tubes right side out and press. Top-stitch along the fold.

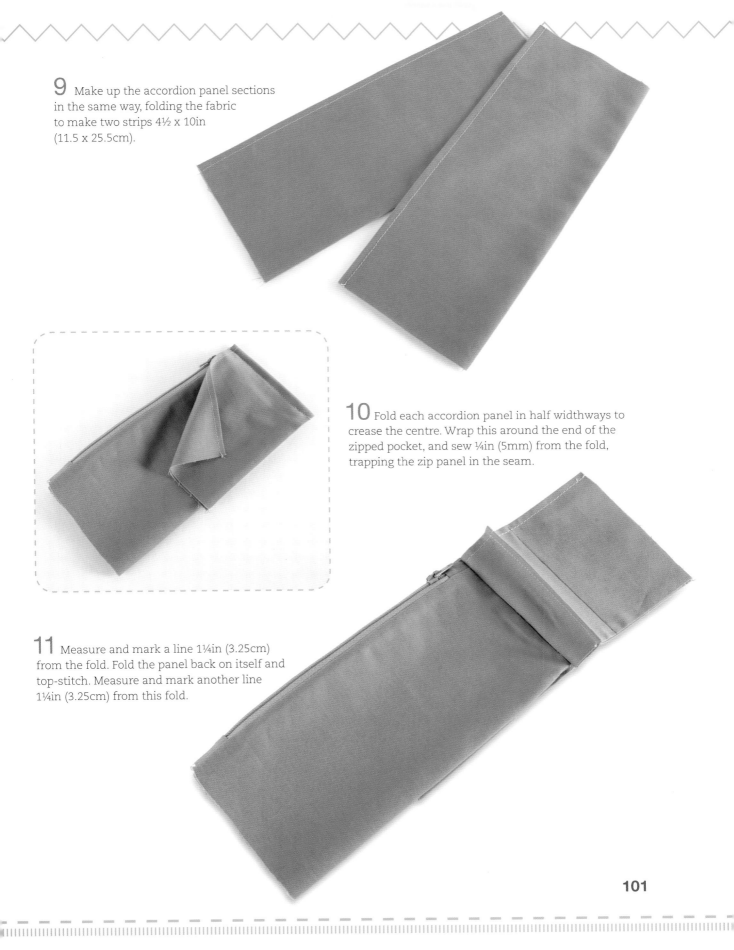

9 Make up the accordion panel sections in the same way, folding the fabric to make two strips 4½ x 10in (11.5 x 25.5cm).

10 Fold each accordion panel in half widthways to crease the centre. Wrap this around the end of the zipped pocket, and sew ¼in (5mm) from the fold, trapping the zip panel in the seam.

11 Measure and mark a line 1¼in (3.25cm) from the fold. Fold the panel back on itself and top-stitch. Measure and mark another line 1¼in (3.25cm) from this fold.

12 Place one of the dividers on the marked line, wrap the accordion panel around the edge and top-stitch ¼in (5mm) from the fold. Mark 1¼in (3.25cm) from this fold, make another fold in the opposite direction and top-stitch, as shown.

13 Repeat with the opposite side of the accordion panel. Starting with the zipped panel, repeat the folding and stitching with the remaining end of the accordion section. Then repeat for the other side of the purse.

14 Take the outer fabric and lining, place wrong sides together and adhere with repositionable spray adhesive. Measure and mark a line 4in (10cm) from the bottom and sew. Place the accordion section over the sewn line on the lining side, then sew the raw accordian edges to the sides of the purse, with a narrow seam allowance, creating your four equally-sized accordian pockets.

VIDEO
Applying bias binding

15 Apply bias binding all around the edge of the purse, mitring the corners as you sew.

Tip

Sew a strip of ribbon inside the purse with a ring on the end to keep your door/locker key to hand!

Blooming Marvellous Tote

Say it with flowers with this pretty summer tote: it's a simple bag to make, but the hexagon roses add an impressive touch. Try to make each flower slightly different to create a quirky, unique look.

Finished size

11½ x 8½in (29.25 x 21.5cm), not including handles

What you need

20 x 18in (50.5 x 46cm) checked fabric

24 x 9½in (61 x 24cm) lining fabric

Six strips of fabric in coordinating colours, each 2½ x 45in (6.5 x 114.5cm)

20 x 18in (50.5 x 46cm) wadding/batting

12 x 7in (30.5 x 18cm) sew-in stabilizer (you could use a lightweight cotton)

14 x 10in (35.5 x 25.5cm) calico for the hexagons: this won't be seen so a plain cotton fabric could be used

3in (7.5cm) hexagon template (see page 128)

Magnetic clasp

Temporary fabric glue stick and spray adhesive

Cut

Two pieces of checked fabric and two pieces of wadding/batting measuring 12 x 9in (30.5 x 23cm)

Two pieces of checked fabric for the handles measuring 18 x 4in (45.75 x 10cm)

Two pieces of wadding/batting measuring 18 x 4in (45.75 x 10cm)

Two pieces of lining, each 12 x 9½in (30.5 x 24cm)

Ten hexagons from calico

Ten 1in (2.5cm) squares of fabric from the strips

Cut the remainder of the strips of fabric in half lengthways, fold in half and press

VIDEO

Making fabric roses

1   Place a 1in (2.5cm) square of fabric in the centre of each hexagon; fix with a dot of glue. Vary the colours of the roses by starting some with dark shades of fabric in the centre and light around the edge, and some with a light centre going to dark around the edge. This is my darkest fabric.

2   Cut three 1½in (4cm) pieces of the next shade of fabric from the folded strip, sew in an overlapping triangle shape over the centre piece of fabric with the folds facing the centre.

3   Cut four 1½in (4cm) pieces from the next shade of folded fabric, and again, folds facing the centre, sew, overlapping the ends. Make sure you cover the stitches from the previous petals.

4   Cut five 2in (5cm) strips for the next round of petals and sew in the same way, then add six strips for the final layer. This time, fix the fabric with your glue stick, turn over and machine stitch close to the edge of the hexagon. Trim away the excess fabric.

5 Arrange the finished hexagons so that they cover the bottom left-hand corner of the checked bag front – you will need to cut some in half.

6 Sew the hexagons right sides together, starting and ending your stitching ¼in (5mm) from the edge of the fabric. When you come to sewing the 'Y' seam where three hexagons meet, fold the fabric out of the way to enable your needle to get right up to the point where the three seams meet. Persevere here as the fabric layers make the hexagons quite thick. Take your stabilizer and sew right sides together with the top of the hexagon panel. Snip off the corners and into the 'V' where the hexagons join, being careful not to cut through the stitches. Turn right side out and press.

7 Attach each checked piece to a piece of wadding/batting using spray adhesive. Pin the hexagon panel over the bottom left-hand corner of one checked piece and hand sew across the top edge using slip stitch. I prefer to hand sew this part, firstly so that the stitches aren't seen, and secondly because the fabric is so thick it can be difficult to get it under the machine!

8 Take the two lining pieces and attach one half of the magnetic clasp to each side, centrally, 1½in (4cm) from the top.

9 To make the handles, place each piece of handle fabric on top of the corresponding wadding/batting, fold each long side to the centre then fold in half lengthways and press. Top-stitch along both sides. Tack/baste the handles to each top side of the checked fabric, facing downwards, 3in (7.5cm) from each side. Sew the top of each checked piece right sides together to the top of a lining piece.

10 Sew the two halves of the bag right sides together, matching lining to lining and outer to outer, leaving a turning gap of about 5in (13cm) in the bottom of the lining. Snip off the corners, turn right side out and sew the turning gap closed.

11 Push the lining inside the bag and press. As the lining was cut slightly longer than the outer fabric, you'll see a border of lining around the top.

Tip
Why not cover one whole side of the bag in blooms? Your bag will look amazing!

Blooming Marvellous Purse

This purse is a good size for a cosmetic bag or phone holder; you could add a chain to the D-ring or make your own wristlet from the instructions for Mini Miss Messenger on page 54.

Finished size

6 x 6in (15.25 x 15.25cm)

What you need

6½ x 4½in (16.5 x 15cm) checked fabric
13 x 13in (33 x 33cm) plain fabric
6½ x 6½in (16.5 x 16.5cm) wadding/batting
8in (20.5cm) zip
½in (1cm) D-ring
6in (15.25cm) ribbon
4in (10cm) square of calico (or plain cotton fabric)
4in (10cm) square of sew-in stabilizer
Four strips of coordinating fabrics measuring 2½ x 10in (6.5 x 25.5cm): I used a piece of the checked fabric for one of my strips
One 1in (2.5cm) square of patterned fabric
Fabric glue stick
3in (7.5cm) hexagon and leaf templates (see page 128)

Cut

One piece of checked fabric measuring 6½ x 4½in (16.5 x 11.5cm)
One piece of plain fabric measuring 6½ x 4½in (16.5 x 11.5cm)
One piece of wadding/batting measuring 6½ x 4½in (16.5 x 11.5cm)
Two pieces of plain fabric measuring 6½ x 2in (16.5 x 5cm)
One piece of wadding/batting measuring 6½ x 2in (16.5 x 5cm)
Two pieces of plain fabric measuring 6½ x 6½in (16.5 x 16.5cm)
Two leaves from plain fabric using your template
One hexagon from calico using your template
2 x 2in (5 x 5cm) plain fabric for the tab

1 Make up a rose hexagon following the instructions for the Blooming Marvellous Tote on page 105. Place the hexagon right sides together with the stabilizer and sew all around the edge. Snip off the corners, make a cut in the centre of the stabilizer and turn right side out. Press.

2 Place the checked fabric over the same size piece of wadding/batting. Position the leaves, slightly overlapping, to the centre right of the fabric and secure with your glue stick. Satin stitch all around the edge and add a stitched 'vein' down the centre of each leaf.

3 Dot a little glue on the back of the hexagon and place to the left of the leaves, overlapping slightly. Hand sew in place with slip stitch.

4 Sew the zip right sides together to the top of the checked fabric piece. You'll notice I like to use a zip that's too long and trim it later – it makes it easier to sew in with the slider out of the way!

5 Place one of the 2in (5cm) strips of plain fabric over its wadding/batting, and sew right sides together to the top side of the zip. Sew the remaining 2in (5cm) and 4½in (11.5cm) plain pieces to the opposite sides of the zip, sandwiching the zip in the centre. Make up the tab by folding the sides of the fabric to the centre, then fold in half and press. Top-stitch along both sides. Thread this through the D-ring and tack/baste, facing inwards to the side of the purse, ½in (1cm) away from the zip. The tab fabric will need to be trimmed – I find it easier to sew a longer piece and cut it back, as small pieces of fabric can be a bit fiddly!

6 Take one plain piece of fabric and place right sides together with the zip section. Sew straight across the bottom. Pin the second lining piece to the opposite side so that the zipped section is sandwiched in the centre, then sew round the edges, leaving a turning gap in the bottom of about 3in (7.5cm). Remove the pins and snip off the corners.

7 Turn right side out, sew the turning gap closed and press. Tie your piece of ribbon onto the D-ring.

Tip
You could pop a little toy filler under the flower to give it a three-dimensional effect! You could also try sewing two flowers together with a loop of ribbon between them to make a bag charm.

Twisted Threads Bag

The idea for the trim on this bag came from a basket of thread and yarn I've been collecting over the years. The colours and textures I was accumulating looked so exciting as I unknotted them and laid them out, and I saw an interesting new fabric developing. Couching is traditionally a way of hand sewing threads over fabric, but for those of us who are a little impatient, this method of machine sewing with a zigzag stitch will give you a quicker result!

Finished size

20½ x 13½in (52 x 34.25cm), not including handles

What you need

46 x 18in (117 x 45.75cm) outer fabric: I've used a wool blend; if you're using cotton you may wish to fuse fleece to the wrong side to give it more stability

46 x 15in (117 x 38.25cm) lining fabric

An assortment of thread, yarn, roving wool and ribbon: enough to cover an area of 13 x 8in (33 x 20.5cm)

16 x 12in (41 x 30.5cm) calico or scrap fabric

16 x 12in (41 x 30.5cm) fusible stabilizer

52in (132cm) of 1in (2.5cm) wide bias binding: I used 26in (66cm) each of two different colours

8in (20.5cm) circle template

Embroidery thread to decorate the handles

Three buttons

Cut

Two pieces of outer fabric measuring 23 x 10½in (58.5 x 26.75cm)

Two pieces of lining fabric measuring 23 x 10½in (58.5 x 26.75cm)

Two pieces of outer fabric measuring 12 x 4½in (30.5 x 11.5cm) for the top panel

Two pieces of lining fabric measuring 12 x 4½in (30.5 x 11.5cm)

Two pieces of outer fabric for the handles measuring 3 x 23in (7.5 x 58.5cm)

Four strips of bias binding each measuring 13in (33cm)

1 Fuse the stabilizer to the back of the calico. Mark out an area of 13 x 8in (33 x 20.5cm) on the right side of the calico. Cut strips of yarn and ribbon to approximately 10in (25.5cm) in length; with the roving wool, tear pieces from the skein instead of cutting, then twist them to form the strips.

2 Place the yarn, one strip at a time, over the marked area and sew with a wide zigzag stitch on your sewing machine. I've used the same colour thread for each piece, but you could change colour if you wish. Continue until the whole area is covered, and don't worry about making your rows too uniform or neat! A quick tip: if there are small gaps in between the rows of yarn, use an alcohol or fabric ink pen to colour in the calico. Apply heat from an iron to set the ink.

3 Cut two panels from this embroidered section, each measuring 12 x 3in (30.5 x 7.5cm). Sew bias binding to the top and bottom of each strip.

4 Use your circle template to trim a curve around the bottom corners of the outer and lining pieces. Sew two rows of stitches across the top of each piece with a long stitch and loose tension on your machine, then pull the bottom thread to gather until the length measures the same as the top panel (12in/30.5cm).

5 Sew the panel to the gathered edge of the bag, right sides facing. Repeat with the lining pieces.

6 Sew the threaded panel to the top section of the bag. I've chosen to hand sew using slip stitch so that the stitches aren't seen, but you could machine sew if you prefer. Trim the ends of the bias binding.

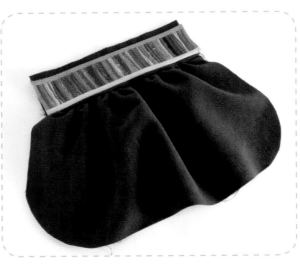

Tip
Add a magnetic clasp to the lining in step 5 if you'd like the bag to stay closed.

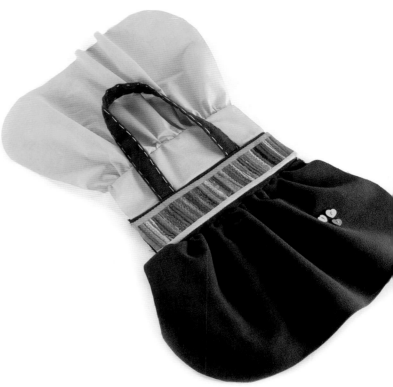

7 Fold then sew the long edges of the handle fabric right sides together to make two tubes. Turn right side out and press, then embroider along each edge with a long running stitch.

8 Tack/baste a handle to each top panel, aligning the raw edges, 2½in (6.5cm) from each side. Sew the top of a lining piece to the top of each outer piece. Sew the three buttons to one side of the bag front.

9 Pin, then sew both bag sections right sides together, matching outer to outer and lining to lining. Leave a turning gap of about 5in (13cm) in the bottom of the lining and make sure the handles are out of the way as you sew. Remove the pins, turn right side out and sew the opening closed. Push the lining inside the bag, press, then top-stitch around the top opening.

Twisted Threads Purse

This envelope-style coin purse would be ideal for a repair kit. Make a gift of it and fill with threads, pins and needles, a small pair of scissors and some mending tape.

Finished size

4 x 4in (10 x 10cm)

What you need

12in (30.5cm) square of calico
12in (30.5cm) square of lining fabric
Assortment of yarns, roving wool, ribbon and embroidery thread: enough to cover an area of 12in (30.5cm) square
2in (5cm) elastic cord (an elastic hair tie is ideal)
Four buttons (including one large flat button)
A piece of paper measuring 8 x 9½in (20.5 x 24cm) to make a template
2in (5cm) circle template (I used a large button)

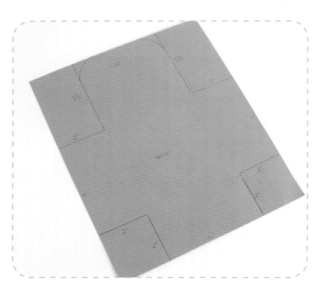

1 Firstly make the paper template. Draw a box at each bottom corner of your paper measuring 2in (5cm) square. Draw a box at each top corner measuring 2in (5cm) wide by 3½in (9cm). The centre top section will form the flap of the purse: use your circle template to round off the corners of the flap, as shown.

2 Cut out the template, place over the calico and draw around the edge. Cut the yarn and wool into strips long enough to cover the drawn area and sew, one by one, over the calico using a zigzag stitch on your machine.

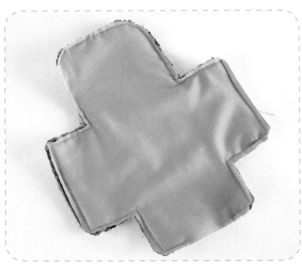

3 Draw around the template again on the back of the fabric and cut out; repeat with the lining fabric.

4 Loop your elastic hair tie and tack/baste, facing inwards, to the centre top of the flap. Pin, then sew the outer and lining pieces right sides together, leaving a turning gap of approximately 2in (5cm) in one side. Snip off the outer corners and into the inner corners. Trim the curved flap with pinking shears.

5 Turn right side out and press. Sew the opening closed with a ladder stitch (see page 15).

6 Fold the sides of the cut-out corners together and hand sew to form a box shape.

7 Fold the sides of the purse to the centre, then fold the base, followed by the flap. Press flat. Sew two buttons together to the centre bottom of the purse so that the elastic wraps around them to close the purse. I prefer to add the buttons at this stage to make sure they are in the correct position. Sew two more buttons to the flap to decorate.

8 Although the purse is quite small, there's plenty of room for coins, notes or a small sewing kit!

Tip

Make up the purse in plain fabric, using interfacing to stiffen the fabric slightly, and add a ribbon tie instead of an elastic hair tie to fasten.

Girl on the Go Bag

A busy girl needs to keep her hands free when she's shopping, eating or dancing, so keep your necessary items in this stylish backpack and off you go!

1 Take the two faux leather flap pieces and the wadding/batting flap piece and, using your circle template, cut the bottom two corners of each piece into curves. Adhere the wadding/batting to the wrong side of the front of the flap with repositionable spray adhesive.

Finished size

9 x 13in (23 x 33cm)

What you need

24 x 10in outer fabric (61 x 25.5cm): I've used a houndstooth check wool

36 x 15in (91.5 x 38cm) lining fabric

44 x 16in (112 x 41cm) faux leather (or contrast fabric if you prefer)

32 x 15in (81.5 x 38cm) wadding/batting

8in (20.5cm) circle template

Twist lock

Four 1in (2.5cm) rectangular rings

Two 1in (2.5cm) rectangular sliders

Repositionable spray fabric adhesive

Wet fabric glue

Fabric clips: you'll find these easier to use than pins on thick fabric

Cut

Two strips of faux leather for the straps measuring 32 x 4in (81.25 x 10cm)

Two pieces of outer fabric measuring 12 x 10in (30.5 x 25.5cm)

Two pieces of faux leather for the base measuring 12 x 4in (30.5 x 10cm)

Two pieces of faux leather for the top measuring 12 x 2in (30.5 x 5cm)

Two pieces of wadding/batting measuring 12 x 15in (30.5 x 38cm)

Two pieces of lining fabric measuring 12 x 15in (30.5 x 38cm)

Two pieces of faux leather for the flap measuring 9 x 8in (23 x 20.5cm)

One piece of wadding/batting for the flap measuring 9 x 8in (23 x 20.5cm)

Four strips of faux leather for the tabs measuring 3 x 4in (7.5 x 10cm)

One piece of lining fabric for the inside pockets measuring 12 x 12in (30.5 x 30.5cm)

3 Make up the straps by folding the two long edges of the strips of faux leather to the centre, fold the short ends inwards, then fold in half lengthways again. Top-stitch along both long sides. As faux leather doesn't crease easily and is thick to pin, spray the wrong sides with adhesive before folding to hold in place as you sew.

2 Sew the two flap pieces right sides together, leaving the straight side open. Turn right side out and top-stitch around the seam. Fit the ring side of the twist lock centrally to the flap, 1in (2.5cm) from the curved end (see page 20).

4 Make up four tabs by folding and sewing the faux leather in the same way. Take two of the tab strips, thread each through a rectangular ring, fold the ends together and secure with a dot of wet glue. Hold with a clip until the glue is dry.

5 Take the two base pieces of faux leather and cut a 1in (2.5cm) square from each bottom corner.

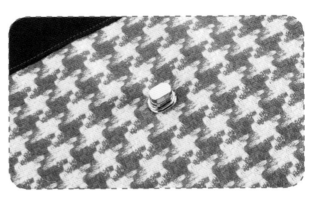

6 Sew one bottom piece right sides together to the bottom of an outer piece of fabric, then sew a top piece right sides together to the top. Crease the seams open with your fingers, then top-stitch along them. Adhere a piece of wadding/batting to the wrong side of this panel, then trim to the same shape.

7 Fit the second half of the twist lock to the front of the bag, centrally, 4½in (11.5cm) from the top.

8 Use this panel as a template to trim the two large lining pieces. Next, take the inside pocket fabric and fold in half, right sides together, then sew along the long open edge to make a tube. Turn right side out and press, then top-stitch along the top folded edge. Pin to one side of the lining, 4in (10cm) from the top, sew around the bottom and sides, then sew straight down the centre to divide in two. Remove the pins.

9 Take the two straps, thread one end of each through a rectangular ring, fold over and sew in a box shape. Tack/baste the two tabs you've already attached rings to, to the bottom of the remaining outer fabric, 1in (2.5cm) from either side. Thread the remaining tabs through the rings attached to the ends of the straps, and tack/baste to the top of the outer fabric, 4in (10cm) from each side. Sew the bottom and top faux-leather pieces right sides together to the top and bottom of the outer fabric, crease the seams open and top-stitch.

10 Adhere the wadding/batting to the wrong side of the back of the bag, then trim away the bottom corners. The opposite ends of the straps are threaded through the sliders, then through the rings on the bottom tabs and back through the sliders. Fold the ends of the straps over and sew. Clip the flap right sides together to the centre top of the bag.

11 Tack/sew the flap in place. Sew a lining piece to the top of each outer piece, attaching the lining with the pocket to the back of the bag.

12 Pin the two bag pieces right sides together, matching the lining pieces and the outer pieces, and sew all the way round, leaving out the cut-out corners and leaving a turning gap of about 4in (10cm) in the bottom of the lining. Remove the pins. Pinch the cut-out corners so that the side seams sit over the base seams, and sew to make the bag base square.

13 Turn right side out, sew the opening closed, push the lining inside the bag and top-stitch around the top edge.

Girl on the Go Purse

This useful zippered pouch slips over the wrist to keep your hands free and your valuables secure. Large enough to hold loose change and a mobile phone, this purse would make a perfect make-up bag too!

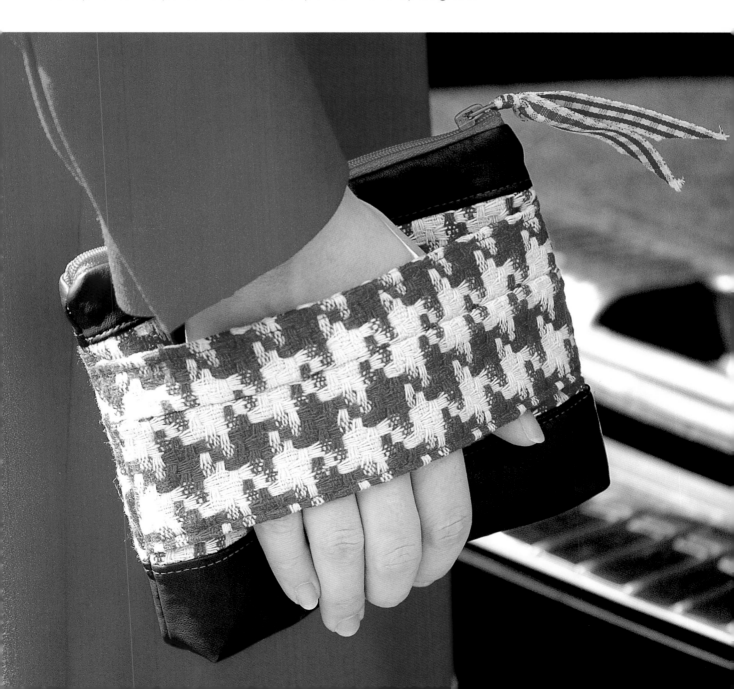

Finished size

7½ x 5½in (19 x 14cm)

What you need

8 x 8in (20.5 x 20.5cm) square of faux leather

8 x 13in (20.5 x 33cm) outer fabric

8 x 13in (20.5 x 33cm) wadding/batting

13 x 8in (33 x 20.5cm) lining fabric

9in (23cm) zip

6in (15.25cm) ribbon

Repositionable spray fabric adhesive

Cut

Two strips of faux leather for the top measuring 8 x 1½in (20.5 x 4cm)

Two strips of faux leather for the bottom measuring 8 x 2½in (20.5 x 6.5cm)

Two pieces of outer fabric measuring 8 x 3½in (20.5 x 9cm)

One piece of outer fabric for the strap measuring 8 x 6in (20.5 x 15.25cm)

Two pieces of lining fabric and two pieces of wadding/batting measuring 8 x 6½in (20.5 x 16.5cm)

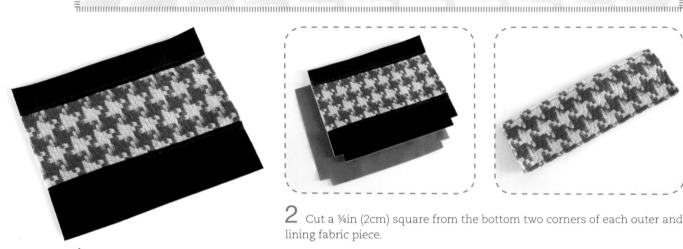

1 Sew the top and bottom faux leather strips right sides together to the top and bottom of the outer fabric pieces. Top-stitch along the seams. Adhere the wadding/batting to the wrong side of each piece with spray adhesive.

2 Cut a ¾in (2cm) square from the bottom two corners of each outer and lining fabric piece.

3 Fold the strap fabric in half lengthways with right sides together, and sew along the long open edge to make a tube. Turn right side out and press with the seam in the centre. Top-stitch along both long edges.

4 Place over the centre panel of the back of the purse and tack/baste along each end.

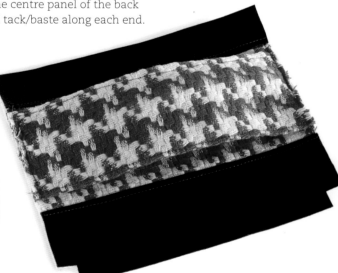

Tip

Faux leather and laminated fabrics can 'stick' to the presser foot on your machine, so use a non-stick foot to help the fabric glide.

5 With the zipper foot on your machine, sew the zip, slider side down, to the top of the purse. Sew the lining to the opposite side of the zip tape.

6 Repeat with the remaining outer and lining pieces. Trim the zip, then hand-sew the open end of the zip closed – this will help to keep the zip in position when constructing the purse.

7 With the zip open, fold the fabric pieces so that the outer and linings are right sides together, pin, then sew all the way round, leaving the cut-out corners and a gap in the bottom of the lining of about 3in (7.5cm) for turning. As you approach the zip, push it towards the lining side. Remove the pins. Pinch the cut-out corners so that the side seams sit over the bottom seams and sew. Turn right side out and sew the opening closed.

8 Push the lining inside the purse. Fold the ribbon in half, thread through the hole in the zip pull and knot. Trim the ribbon if necessary.

Templates | Index

All the templates are given at actual size.

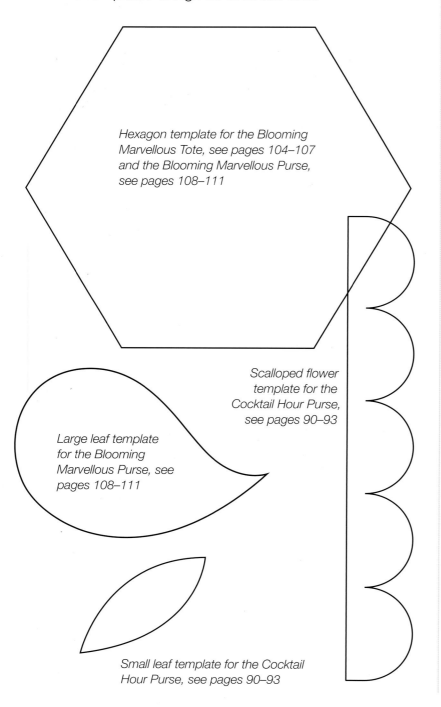

Hexagon template for the Blooming Marvellous Tote, see pages 104–107 and the Blooming Marvellous Purse, see pages 108–111

Scalloped flower template for the Cocktail Hour Purse, see pages 90–93

Large leaf template for the Blooming Marvellous Purse, see pages 108–111

Small leaf template for the Cocktail Hour Purse, see pages 90–93